SIGNS OF THE INK

The Linda Schele Series in Maya and Pre-Columbian Studies

This series was made possible through the generosity of
William C. Nowlin, Jr., and Bettye H. Nowlin
The National Endowment for the Humanities
and the following donors:

Elliot M. Abrams and AnnCorinne Freter

Anthony Alofsin

Joseph W. Ball and Jennifer T. Taschek

William A. Bartlett

Elizabeth P. Benson

Boeing Gift Matching Program

William W. Bottorff

Victoria Bricker

Robert S. Carlsen

Frank N. Carroll

Roger J. Cooper

Susan Glenn

John F. Harris

Peter D. Harrison

Joan A. Holladay

Marianne J. Huber

Jānis Indrikis

The Institute for Mesoamerican Studies

Anna Lee Kahn

Rex and Daniela Koontz

Christopher and Sally Lutz

Judith M. Maxwell

Joseph Orr

The Patterson Foundation

John M. D. Pohl

Mary Anna Prentice

Philip Ray

Louise L. Saxon

David M. and Linda R. Schele

Richard Shiff

Ralph E. Smith

Barbara L. Stark

Penny J. Steinbach

Carolyn Tate

Barbara and Dennis Tedlock

Nancy Troike

Donald W. Tuff

Javier Urcid

Barbara Voorhies

E. Michael Whittington

Sally F. Wiseley, M.D.

Judson Wood, Jr.

SIGNS OF THE **INKA KHIPU**

BINARY CODING

IN THE ANDEAN KNOTTED-STRING RECORDS

Gary Urton

 UNIVERSITY OF TEXAS PRESS, AUSTIN

First edition, 2003

Requests for permission to reproduce material from
this work should be sent to Permissions, University
of Texas Press, Box 7819, Austin, TX 78713-7819.

♾ The paper used in this book meets the minimum
requirements of ANSI/NISO Z39.48-1992 (R1997)
(Permanence of Paper).

Library of Congress Cataloging-in-Publication Data
Urton, Gary, date
Signs of the Inka Khipu : binary coding in the
Andean knotted-string records / Gary Urton.
    p.   cm. — (The Linda Schele series in Maya
and pre-Columbian studies)
Includes bibliographical references and index.
ISBN 0-292-78539-9 (alk. paper)
ISBN 0-292-78540-2 (pbk.: alk. paper)
1. Quipu.   2. Incas—Communication.   3. Binary
system (Mathematics)   I. Title.   II. Series.
F3429.3.Q6 U78   2003
302.2'22—dc21
                                2002012297

For Anthony Aveni and Jane Pinchin,
dear friends and colleagues
and unwavering sources of support
for many years at Colgate University

Contents

He who seeks to count the stars before he can count the scores and knots of the *quipus* deserves derision.

GARCILASO DE LA VEGA,
Royal Commentaries of the Incas
(1966 [1609–1617]: 397)

The author, who over twenty years ago published a book on Quechua and Inka astronomy entitled *At the Crossroads of the Earth and the Sky: An Andean Cosmology,* fervently hopes that his reader of today will be more sympathetic to the present undertaking than would have been the Inca Garcilaso de la Vega, who penned the above admonishment almost four centuries ago!

Preface and Acknowledgments

In one form or another, I have been at work on this book for almost ten years. The basic argument that I present here began to take shape in a paper entitled "What Do the Khipu Tell Us about the Inka Empire?" which I delivered in a symposium that was held at Dumbarton Oaks, Washington, D.C., in 1997. The symposium "Expressions of Power in the Inka Empire," in which the original paper was presented, was organized by Richard Burger, Ramiro Matos M., and Craig Morris. I thank the organizers of that symposium for the opportunity to present a paper in what was the first and only symposium on the Inka ever to be held in the important venue of Dumbarton Oaks.

The paper from the Dumbarton Oaks symposium sat for a couple of years before being taken out, dusted off, and presented in a significantly revised form at a conference entitled "First Writing," which was organized by Stephen D. Houston and held at the Sundance resort in Provo, Utah, on April 6–8, 2000. I thank Steve for the invitation to participate in that wonderful conference, and I also thank him and the other participants for their questions and comments on my paper. I note that a condensed version of the arguments and some of the material presented in Chapters 1–5 of this book are scheduled to be published as a chapter in a volume entitled *The First Writing* (Cambridge University Press, in press), currently being edited by Houston from the papers presented at the Sundance conference.

In a parallel telling of the history of how this book came into being, I should also note that this work is perhaps the most prominent result of a decade-long interchange with my colleague Bill Conklin. My first opportunity to look closely at a collection of khipu came in 1992 when Conklin and I spent a day studying and discussing khipu in the collections of the American Museum of Natural History in New York City. My first attempt at an analysis of the issues addressed in this book—specifically its concern with the possible meaning of several features of binary coding (i.e., spinning, plying, and knot directionality) in the khipu—appeared in an article published in 1994, which was based on my independent study of the large collection of khipu in the Museum für Völkerkunde in Berlin. The material presented in that article subsequently came under intense scrutiny and further analysis by Conklin in an article that he originally wrote and presented at a round table on the khipu, which was co-organized by Jeffrey Quilter and myself and took place at Dumbarton Oaks in 1997 (see Conklin 2002). I am now returning in this study to the topic of binary coding, but I do so with the advantage of Conklin's sharp insights and clear thinking in his recent article, as well as on the basis of additional observations that I have recorded in the intervening period.

For their reading of earlier versions of parts of the material presented in this book, I thank Anthony Aveni, Carrie Brezine, Bill Conklin, Robert Harberts, and Camilla Townsend. Special thanks go to my longtime friend Robert Harberts, of the Goddard Space Center, for discussing with me the information storage capacity of the khipu binary coding system. The two readers for the University of Texas Press, Frank Salomon and Stephen Houston, provided exceptionally clear, critical, and comprehensive commentary on the manuscript; I thank them both for the time and energy they put into helping to improve this book. I thank Laura Sanchis of Colgate University's Computer Science Department for her helpful suggestions on readings in binary coding, and I thank my former student Nicole Casi, both for reading an early, partial manuscript of the book as well as for reminding me of the stones. Thanks to my wife, Julia Meyerson, who read and commented on the entire manuscript and who produced the drawings. And finally, I express my gratitude to my editor at the University of Texas Press, Nancy Warrington, whose care and attention in editing the manuscript were greatly appreciated. I alone am responsible for any errors that remain in this book.

For access to and help with my study of khipu in the Museum für Völkerkunde in Berlin in 1993, I thank Drs. Manuela Fischer and Marie Gaida. For similar assistance and collegial support in the American Museum of Natural History in New York on three different occasions (1992, 1996, and 2000), I thank Craig Morris, Vuka Roussakis, Barbara

Conklin, and Anahid Akasheh. For their support and cooperation dur-
ing my study of khipu in the Peabody Museum for Archaeology and
Ethnology at Harvard University, I thank Gloria P. Greis and Bill Fash.
Anne Rowe made possible my study of two khipu samples in the Textile
Museum in Washington, D.C.

My study of the khipu in the Centro Mallqui, Leymebamba (Chachapoyas), Peru, was made possible by the generosity of Sonia Guillén
and Adriana von Hagen and by the goodwill and indefatigable good
spirits of my "warmi khipukamayuqkuna": Marcelita Hidalgo, Empera-
triz Alvarado, Acelita Portal, and Rosalía Choque. I also acknowledge
with gratitude the able assistance in Leymebamba of Alejo Rojas, an
archaeology student from San Marcos University in Lima, in 1999.

My ethnographic fieldwork in Candelaria and Tarabuco, Bolivia, in
1993–1994, which I draw on here for material concerning the symbolism of colors in dyeing threads and weaving textiles, was facilitated by
my dear friends Verónica Cereceda and the late Gabriel Martínez, who
generously allowed me to use the facilities and contacts of their NGO,
Antropólogos Sur Andino (ASUR), which focused on the promotion
of weaving among women of the region of Sucre, Bolivia.

For their financial support of my research over the years since 1993,
I thank the following organizations, foundations, and individuals: the
German Academic Exchange Service (DAAD), for research support in
Berlin, Germany, in the summer of 1993; the National Endowment
for the Humanities, for a Summer Stipend for work in Berlin and at
the Archivo General de Indias in Seville in the summer of 1993, as
well as for postdoctoral fellowships to conduct and write up khipu research in 1994–1995 and 2000; the National Science Foundation, for a
postdoctoral grant (#SBR 9221737) for research on Quechua ethnomathematics in Sucre, Bolivia, in 1993–1994; the Wenner-Gren Foundation for Anthropological Research, for support of my research on the
khipu from Laguna de los Cóndores, Chachapoyas, in the summer of
1999; the Dean of the Faculty, Colgate University, for support for my
research in Chachapoyas in the summer of 1998 and at the Peabody Museum in 2000; the American Philosophical Society, for a grant to conduct research in the Archivo General de Indias in Seville, Spain, in 2000;
and finally, to the John D. and Catherine T. MacArthur Foundation, for
support for research and time off to write up my studies on the khipu
(including this book) in 2001–2006.

SIGNS OF THE INKA KHIPU

CHAPTER 1

Memory, Writing, and Record Keeping in the Inka Empire

It is one of the great ironies of the age in which we live that the cacophony of computer-based, electronically produced information that suffuses our every waking moment is carried into our consciousness on patterned waves of just two signs: *1* and *0*. This, of course, is no news. We have all been made aware since the dawn of the present Information Age that the ongoing revolution in computing technology rests on a system of binary coding. I discuss the matter at length below, but I would clarify here that by "binary coding," I mean a system of communication based on units of information that take the form of strings of signs or signals, each individual unit of which represents one or the other of a pair of alternative (usually opposite) identities or states; for example, the signal may be on or off (as in a light switch), positive or negative (as in an electrical current), or 1 or 0 (as in computer coding). One can argue that it is the simplicity of binary coding that gives computing technology and its information systems their great flexibility and seemingly inexhaustible expansiveness. In this study, I explore an earlier and potentially equally powerful system of coding information that was at home in pre-Columbian South America and which, like the coding systems used in present-day computer language, was structured primarily as a binary code.

After the above grandiose introduction, it may come as a letdown to the reader to learn that we do not yet know, in fact, how to interpret or read the majority of the information that is presumably encoded in the recording system that I describe and analyze in this book. The system in question is that of the Inka khipu.[1] *Khipu* (knot; to knot) is a term drawn from Quechua, the lingua franca and language of administration of the Inka Empire (ca. 1450–1532 C.E.). The khipu were knotted-

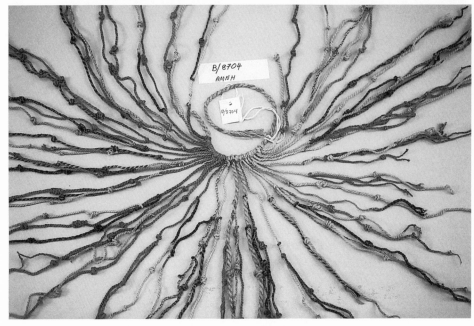

1.1. A khipu in the American Museum of Natural History (AMNH B/8704).

string devices (see Figure 1.1) that were used for recording both statistical and narrative information, most notably by the Inka but also by other peoples of the central Andes from pre-Inkaic times (see Conklin 1982; Shady, Narváez, and López 2000), through the colonial and republican eras (Brokaw 1999; Murra 1975; Platt 2002; Urton 1998, 2001), and even—in a considerably transformed and attenuated form—down to the present day (Mackey 1970, 2002; Núñez del Prado 1990; Ruiz Estrada 1998; Salomon 2002).

I estimate from my own studies and from the published works of other scholars that there are about 600 extant khipu in public and private collections around the world (see Chapter 2). Although provenience data are notoriously sketchy for museum samples of khipu, what information we do have tends to support the conclusion that most samples were looted from grave sites along the central and south coast of Peru during the late nineteenth and early twentieth centuries. A recent discovery of thirty-two khipu in burial chambers in the northern Peruvian Andes is consistent with the presumed funerary disposal of these devices (see Urton 2001 for a discussion of the possible significance of this context for khipu disposal).

Europeans became aware of the knotted-string devices used by the indigenous Inka record keepers from the earliest days following the Spanish Conquest, which began in 1532. Hernando Pizarro, the brother of the leader of the conquistadors and (later) marquis, Francisco Pizarro, described an encounter that he and his men had with khipu keepers on the royal road from the highlands down to the central coast of Peru in 1533. Pizarro notes that when he and his men removed some goods from one of the Inka storehouses, the record keepers "untied some of the knots which they had in the deposits section [of the khipu], and they [re-]tied them in another section [of the khipu]" (H. Pizarro 1920 [1533]: 175 and 178).

Following this initial reference to khipu, accounts of these devices appear with considerable frequency in the Spanish chronicles and documents recorded throughout the first few decades of the establishment of the colony (see Urton n.d.a). Khipu were one of the principal sources of information used by the Spaniards as they began to compile records pertaining to the former inhabitants of the empire. The former Inka record keepers—known as *khipukamayuq* (knot maker/keeper)—supplied colonial administrators with a tremendous variety and quantity of information pertaining to censuses, tribute, ritual and calendrical organization, genealogies, and other such matters from Inka times. While numerous colonial writers in Peru left accounts of the khipu that inform us on certain features and operations of these devices, none of these accounts is extensive or detailed enough to put us on solid ground in our attempts today to understand exactly how the Inka made and consulted (that is, read) these knotted and dyed records.

An issue of utmost interest and concern to several scholars who are intensively studying these devices today (see esp. Quilter and Urton 2002) centers around the question of whether the khipu recording system should be characterized as a system of "mnemonics," or if it may in fact have constituted a system of "writing." In a word, the matter under dispute is whether khipu were (respectively) string-and-knot-based configurations whose purpose was to provide "cues" to aid the Inka administrator who made any particular sample to recall a specific body of memorized information, or if these devices were constructed with conventionalized units of information that could be read by khipu makers throughout the empire. I should state that I am primarily an adherent of

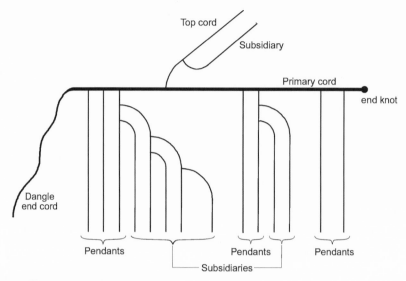

1.2. Khipu construction elements.

the latter of these two starkly differentiated and ultimately caricatured views of khipu records (see Urton 1998, 2002). In fact, I suspect that the final solution we will arrive at regarding the types of information retained on these devices will look more like a combination of the two forms of record keeping alluded to above.

In this introductory chapter, I first provide an overview of these two differing points of view on the question of what kind of recording system the khipu may have represented as they have emerged in publications since the beginning of the twentieth century. I then lay out in a general way the new approach to analyzing and interpreting the khipu developed in this book. Before beginning, it may be helpful to the non-Andeanist reader for me to describe the basic features of these remarkable devices, the khipu.

Khipu Structures

In general terms, khipu are composed of a main, or primary, cord to which are attached a variable number of what are termed pendant strings (see Figure 1.2). Many samples have only a few pendant strings, while a couple have upward of 1,500 pendants. To state definitively the average number of pendant strings on all khipu would be a difficult undertaking, particularly as our studies of some collections are incomplete. As an example, however, I note that for a collection of thirty-two khipu recently discovered in Chachapoyas, in northern Peru (see Urton 2001 and below), the average number of pendant strings on the twenty-two samples that were well enough preserved to allow for close study was 149 (the range is between 6 and 762).

Primary cords usually have a diameter in the range of $1/2$ to $2/3$ cm, and they often display complex bi- or multicolored spin and ply patterns. It is not uncommon for primary cords to be finished off with a "wrapping" composed of a cord made of two or three pairs of differently colored spun and plied yarns (see Figure 1.3). In some cases, tassels may be tied onto primary cords indicating divisions or classifications (of some manner) of the information registered on groups of pendant strings. I have examined some twenty khipu samples in various collections that have large needlework "bundles" that terminate one end of the primary cord (see Figure 1.4). Salomon has described similar bundles on a few samples of khipu used today for ritual purposes in the Peruvian central highland community of Tupicocha (Salomon 2002; see below). Such "end ornaments" in Tupicocha are generally referred to as *pachacamanta* ("about/concerning the hundred"; Salomon 2002: 303). Given that the unit of one hundred tribute payers was an important organizational unit in Inka administration—often used as a synonym for the sociopolitical and communal labor groupings referred to as *ayllu*— these khipu ornaments as retained in the samples from Tupicocha today may offer a clue to the significance of such ornaments on archaeological khipu. That is, they may have indicated the administrative class of khipu in question, as well as its general subject matter and the magnitude of units recorded.

Pendant strings may have attached to them secondary, or subsidiary, strings, which may, in turn, carry subsidiary (i.e., tertiary) strings, and so on.[2] Some khipu also display top strings; these strings are attached in such a way that they leave the primary cord in the opposite direction from the pendant strings. In some cases, the attachment of a top string is by means of a loop that binds the top string into the attachments of a group of pendant strings across the primary cord (see Figure 1.5).

As I discuss in greater detail below, on most khipu, knots of three different types were tied into pendant, subsidiary, and top strings. In the

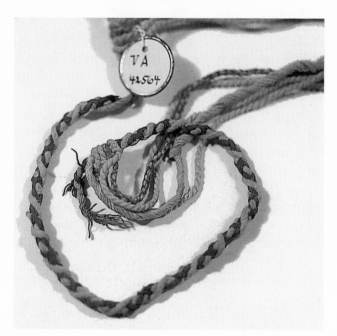

1.3. Primary cord with S wrapping (Museum für Völkerkunde, Berlin, VA 42564).

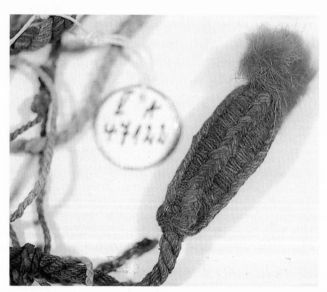

1.4. Needlework "bundle," or "end ornament" (Museum für Völkerkunde, Berlin, VA 47122).

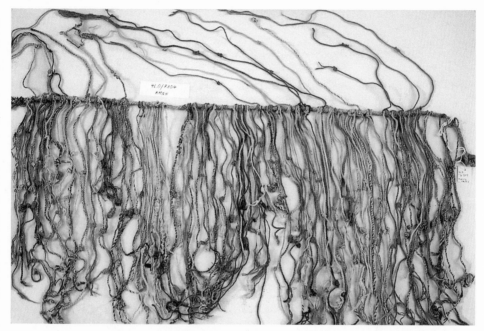

1.5. Khipu with multiple top strings (AMNH 41.0/7304).

case of those khipu that recorded quantitative values (rather than narrative records; see below), the three types of knots are tied in patterned arrangements of clusters along the body of strings to indicate increasingly higher powers of ten (see Figure 1.6; for further overviews of khipu structures and construction techniques, see Arellano 1999; Ascher and Ascher 1969, 1975, 1997 [1981]; Conklin 2002; Loza 1998; Mackey 2002; Mackey et al. 1990; Pereyra 1997, 2001; Radicati di Primeglio 1979; Salomon 2002; and Urton 1994, 2001, 2002).

Some of the features of khipu, such as the decimal arrangement of knots on many samples, are described for us in Spanish accounts written during the colonial era either by Spaniards or by literate Andeans (especially Garcilaso de la Vega and Felipe Guaman Poma de Ayala). For an appreciation of certain characteristics of khipu construction, however, we have had to wait for the results of careful scientific study of museum samples in modern times.

With this understanding of some of the main features of the khipu, we can now turn to the question of the possible nature of the signs encoded on these devices; that is, was this a memory-cueing device? Was it a system of writing? Or was it some other type of record keeping?

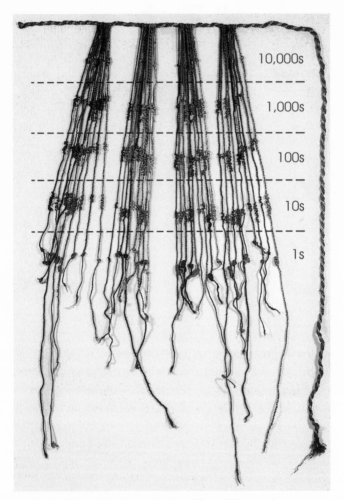

10,000s

1,000s

100s

10s

1s

1.6. Decimal hierarchical organization of knots (Museum für Völkerkunde, Berlin, VA 47083).

Mnemonic Schemes and Devices

I should begin by establishing the parameters to be taken into account in the discussion below of memory and mnemonic devices (for excellent treatments of the nature of memory in Andean societies, past and present, see Kaulicke 2000: 5–10; and Howard 2002). I note, on the one hand, that I set aside from consideration the large body of works relating to the topic of mnemonics undertaken from the psychobiological paradigmatic perspective. Although such studies offer many insights into the capacities and motivations of individual processes of remembering and recalling, my concern here is not with experimental instances of what, when, or how individuals remember, recollect, or otherwise behave with respect to a piece of memorized information. In this regard, I am in agreement with Maurice Halbwachs when he wrote:

> One is rather astonished when reading psychological treatises that deal with memory to find that people are considered there as isolated beings. These make it appear that to understand our mental operations, we need to stick to individuals and first of all, to divide all the bonds which attach individuals to the society of their fellows. Yet it is in society that people normally acquire their memories. It is also in society that they recall, recognize, and localize their memories. (1992 [1941/1952]: 38)

My concern rather is with placing memory, recollection, and recitation in social contexts, as well as with understanding how (i.e., in what manner and with what sociopolitical motives and consequences) people commit information to memory schema, transmit that information to other people, and then interact with others through or in relation to that body of memory-based information. For memory routines, regimes, and forms of interaction of these types, the sociocultural, interactional, and intellectual paradigms directing anthropological theory and practice are, in my view, preferable to those of psychology.

However, I should also state that I am not concerned here with the kinds of issues—at the other end of the spectrum of inclusiveness of human interactions—addressed in Paul Connerton's now classic study *How Societies Remember* (1989). That is, it is not my intent to analyze the kinds of large-scale collective rituals and ceremonies through which community, state, or national values, histories, and identities were formulated, reproduced, and commemorated publicly. Rather, I am concerned with what we may now define as the middle range of the work of memory and notation, that between the individual and the collectivity. This entails both individuals and classes of people (e.g., administrators, historians) within communities who produced and maintained records on such matters as population censuses, tribute (whether paid, projected, or levied), genealogical relations among the living and connections between the living and the dead, mythohistories, and so on.

In most ancient and modern states, such records have been retained in written documents. The big question we will address here is: Were the khipu the "written documents" of the Inka Empire? In addressing this question, we must begin by sorting out the difference and the relationship between mnemonics and writing.

My Merriam Webster's dictionary (1978 [1904]) defines *mnemonics* as: "1. the science or art of improving the memory, as by the use of certain formulas. 2. formulas or other aids to help in remembering." Thus, for instance, the formula that begins "thirty days hath September, April, June, and November" is a mnemonic device that helps me to remember the number of days in the months of the year. Although this formula is generally spoken aloud or under the breath, it can obviously (as above) be written.

Regarding the possible role of formulas in khipu record keeping in Inka times, I strongly suspect that there were configurations of strings, knots, colors, and other features that were linked to, and therefore provided cues for, recitations of formulaic information on the order of the "thirty days" formula described above. By analogy with other settings in which formulas were central elements in very complicated traditions of reciting sagas, epics, and other long memorized narratives (e.g., see Ong 1995 [1982]: 58–60 on the use of formulas in ancient Greek and 1960s–1970s Yugoslavian oral narration), it is reasonable to suppose that formulas may have formed important components of the narrative strategies linked to khipu recitations. Some of these may be at least partially recoverable from close study of colonial chronicles and documents (e.g., Julien 2000), from the few surviving instances of ritualism connected with the display of khipu today (Salomon 2002), as well as from the study of semantic strategies and syntactic structures of Quechua discourse and poetics (e.g., Howard 2002; Howard-Malverde 1990; Mannheim 1998).

Another common type of mnemonic device is the deceptively simple string tied around the finger to help recall some piece of memorized information. In the string-around-the-finger type of memory aid, one first determines the information (e.g., the message or task) one wishes to recall by means of the memory aid. The information is then linked by the mnemonist to a memory-cueing device, which in this case is the piece of string tied around the finger. The person then goes about his/her business, but upon seeing or becoming aware of the extraordinary presence of a string tied around his/her finger—surprise being the trigger for cueing in this particular system—the mnemonist remembers or recites the message, or performs the task, which he/she had arbitrarily connected to the string in tying it around his/her finger.

To explore somewhat further the nature and implications of the string-around-the-finger cueing device, I believe it is fair to say that we generally have the understanding that no one other than the wearer of such a device will know its meaning, unless the wearer indicates the meaning to another person. For instance, if you were to see a string tied around my finger, you might suspect that I was trying to remember something by means of that string; however, you could not know what the content of that message to myself was unless I told it to you. This is because such devices are memory aids; they are generally not composed of signs having conventional values. It is particularly relevant to the issues we are concerned with in this study to note that if I were to forget the information I had originally attached to a string tied around my finger, not even I, its creator, could retrieve the message from looking at the string; this is because there is, as I have said, no information encoded in or on the string.

Another mnemotechnic device bearing a similar information content to the string-around-the-finger type is the rosary. This latter device, composed of beads or other counters strung together on a string, is used as a prompting device; the user runs his or her fingers along the beads while reciting a fixed, memorized formula, or credo. Although the rosary differs from the string around the finger in that the former is linked to complex, shared formulae, whereas the latter is a sort of one-off prompt for a private message, nonetheless, the two devices are similar in one important respect: the message that is prompted by their use is not recorded in (or on) the memory-cueing device itself. That is, the beads are not signs; they are merely place holders. Thus, if the user of either of these memory aids forgets the message that was originally intended to be prompted by the device, the message cannot be recovered from information (i.e., signs with conventionalized meanings) on the object itself. This is because neither of these contrivances is, in fact, a device for record keeping; rather, they are prompts for information stored in the memory of the user(s).

Some colonial commentators (e.g., Molina ["el Cuzqueño"] 1916 [1573]: 23–24), as well as one of the most notable early modern students of the khipu (Locke 1923: 31), suppose that these devices were string-around-the-finger or rosary-type memory aids. If this was the case, then we cannot be sanguine about our prospects for ever reading, or giving an authoritative interpretation of, one of these devices, as all of the native khipu mnemonics specialists of these objects have long since died. However, I believe, and will attempt to demonstrate here, that such a comparison is profoundly inappropriate for several reasons, most notably because the khipu exhibits far greater complexity and patterning in its structure and organization than the rosary or other similar devices (e.g., incised "message sticks," etc.). I return to this comparison in the conclusions, by which time I believe the reader will agree that the comparison between khipu and rosaries and other similar devices is deeply misleading and irrelevant.

A more complicated mnemonic device, but still of the general class we have just been considering, is that of the Medieval "memory theater." This was a mnemonic method whereby a usually large and detailed body of information was keyed to—that is, placed mentally inside of— a complex, often architectural, structure, like a building with multiple rooms with pictures on the walls, for example. When the mnemonist wanted to recall the information, he/she would do so by making a tour of the mental space constructed, retrieving pieces of the narrative that had been placed at certain loci within the structure (see Spence 1984; see also Hasenohr 1982 for a fascinating account of the use of the segments of the hands as a structure for memorizing and recalling information). The principal source on the memory theater is Frances Yates's masterful study *The Art of Memory* (1966; see also Carruthers 1993). Yates details the varied principles behind this combined memory structure and routine, beginning with its earliest forms in the classical Mediterranean world and proceeding to the Renaissance. In the interest of brevity, I provide below an excellent summary of European memory theaters as recounted in Patrick Hutton's *History as an Art of Memory:*

> The art of memory as it was traditionally conceived was based upon associations between a structure of images easily remembered and a body of knowledge in need of organization. The mnemonist's task was to attach the facts that he wished to recall to images that were so

visually striking or emotionally evocative that they could be recalled at will. He then classified these images in an architectural design of places with which he was readily familiar. The landscape of memory so constructed was an imaginary tableau in which a world of knowledge might be contained for ready reference. It was in effect a borrowed paradigm, the logic of whose imaginary structure gave shape to the otherwise formless knowledge he wished to retain. (1993: 27)

We must ask whether or not the memory theater, with its association between a large, complicated body of information organized and attached to places within a complex structural (e.g., architectural) mental image, is an appropriate model to adopt for the kind of "recording" system represented by the khipu. In my reading of certain views of the khipu recording system (see below), it seems that some commentators would answer this question in the affirmative. If this was the case, we would again (i.e., as with the string-around-the-finger or rosary mnemonic devices) be unlikely to be able to retrieve much, if any, information from study of these devices today.

I must say here, however, that I am skeptical about the possibility that the memory theater offers a reasonable model for the intellectual tradition and mnemonic procedures of a recording system in which the structures to which memories would have been projected were actual physical, constructed objects—like the khipu. It is one thing (certainly in social terms) to key memories to a mental image and quite another to key them to a complex, portable fabrication that can be (and was, as we read in the chronicles) carried around, studied and restudied, changed in various ways, and stored away for later referral. We must also ask, if the khipu *was* an empty physical schema onto which memories were projected, why would the khipukamayuq have needed or wanted to construct such objects in the first place? Such a practice seems uncalled for and unreasonable because, first, the record keepers could have accomplished the same ends with a purely mental image, as was done in the European memory theater, since a mental image is even more portable than a khipu! And second, since (according to this interpretation) the khipu would not have contained any actual information in the form of signs with conventionalized values, what use would it have served? The khipukamayuq could not have recovered lost or forgotten information from it, so why make it in the first place?

I should note in regard to these matters that the chronicler Sarmiento de Gamboa, who interviewed and compared the historical accounts of over one hundred khipukamayuq (see Urton 1990: 18–19), made a clear distinction between the work of memorizing historical accounts and recording information on the khipu. That is, Sarmiento first notes that

> . . . to supply the want of letters, these barbarians had a curious invention which was very good and accurate. This was that from one to the other, from fathers to sons, they handed down past events, repeating the story of them many times, just as lessons are repeated from a professor's chair, making the hearers say these historical lessons over and over again until they were fixed in the memory. (Sarmiento de Gamboa 1999 [1572]: 41)

It will be noted that Sarmiento does not suggest that the memorized information is being keyed to khipu by these memory artists. This accords with what we learn from students of oral recitations, who stress that it is versification and repetition, not the reliance on a mnemonic device, that are the keys to memorizing long passages (see Lord 1960; Notopoulos 1938: 469; Ong 1995: 60). To return to Sarmiento's testimony, several lines after the above passage he goes on to say:

> Finally, they recorded, and they still record, the most notable things which consist in their numbers (or statistics), on certain cords called *quipu*, which is the same as to say reasoner or accountant. On these cords they make certain knots by which, and by differences of colour, they distinguish and record each thing as by letters. It is a thing to be admired to see what details may be recorded on these cords, for which there are masters like our writing masters. (1999: 41)

Thus, Sarmiento distinguishes between the work of memorizing long historical narratives, which did not involve the khipu, and that of recording statistical data, apparently with notations giving some manner of contextual information, by means of the khipu. We will see in other sources, however, that the information recorded on the khipu was of a somewhat more complicated nature, more so than is suggested by Sarmiento in the above quotation.

The last example of a form of mnemonics that I review here will, in fact, move us across the border that usually separates mnemonics and writing. I am referring to the sort of memory aid we commonly make for ourselves, such as a notation I might write on my desk calendar: "lunch, John." Were I to see such a notation to myself on my calendar for tomorrow's date, I would know immediately that this pair of words, written in alphabetic script, was a mnemonic for the complete message: "At noon tomorrow, I am scheduled to have lunch with my colleague John Smith." Now, mnemonic messages of almost precisely this level of abstractness (i.e., "lunch, John") make up the majority of the earliest texts written in the cuneiform script, beginning around 3200 B.C.E. As we will see, specialists in cuneiform tend to be quite hesitant about classifying such notations as "writing." This is because, in the earliest cuneiform texts, the sign units making up such mnemonic notations are composed of logograms—that is, nonphonetic word signs—which are generally not classified as "true writing."

In their incisive and highly informative study *Archaic Bookkeeping* (1993), Hans Nissen, Peter Damerow, and Robert Englund lay out in some detail the processes and general line of development through which writing emerged in the ancient Near East. To begin with, and as has been forcefully and persuasively argued by Denise Schmandt-Besserat (1996), the development of true writing in Mesopotamia followed a long period during which notations were made in the form of clay tokens of various types. These token-based accounting and record-keeping traditions began around 9000 B.C.E. and evolved into the first inscribed texts, which appeared around 3200 B.C.E. (Schmandt-Besserat 1996: 117–122). As Nissen, Damerow, and Englund make clear, the earliest written texts generally contain numerical notations as well as a relatively limited number of ideographic signs (i.e., nonphonological logograms):

> Unfortunately, on most of the archaic tablets, in particular on those from script phase Uruk IV [ca. 3100 B.C.E.], the information given is kept as concise as possible. *Everything expected to be known by the reader was omitted by the scribe.* Thus there was obviously no need to elaborate on syntactic relationships, for example, to include extra information about the sender or the receiver of goods involved. It apparently sufficed to report the quantities of the goods in question. The nature of these products was often obvious from the type of numerical signs employed . . . At the end of the text, the name of the

responsible person or institution was added . . . We are thus merely able to detect a relationship between the entries, but not the nature of this relationship. (1993: 20–21; my emphasis)

One such text, dating to script phase Uruk III (ca. 3000 B.C.E.), is shown in Figure 1.7. This text establishes, in some syntactically unspecified manner, a relationship between two cattle and the temple of the goddess Inanna (Nissen, Damerow, and Englund 1993: 21, Fig. 23).

It will be seen that, in terms of the lack of syntactic information in the two notations, the mnemonic text shown in Figure 1.7 is not significantly different from the mnemonic text "lunch, John" that I described earlier as one I might write on my own calendar. However, in terms of the nature of the signs employed in the two inscriptions, there is a profound difference, for the text shown in Figure 1.7 is composed of (nonphonetic) logographic sign units, whereas the signs that I write on

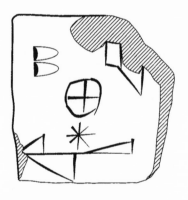

1.7. Mnemonic text in early cuneiform. From *Archaic Bookkeeping: Early Writing and Techniques of Economic Administration in the Ancient Near East* by Hans J. Nissen, Peter Damerow, and Robert K. Englund (University of Chicago Press, 1993). Author's [Hans J. Nissen] original, based on Tablet W21446, now in HD (Uruk Collection of the Deutsches Archäologisches Institute Baghdad in the University of Heidelberg); 44 × 47 × 17 mm; date: archaic script phase Uruk III.

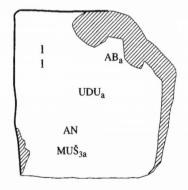

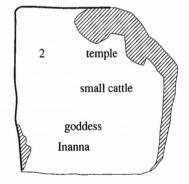

my calendar are phonologically based (i.e., alphabetic) sign units. Yet, I repeat, *both* inscriptions are "mnemonic aids."

We turn now to consider the interpretations of khipu as mnemonic devices. When we encounter (as we shall) references to these knotted-string constructions as "mnemonic devices," we should now insist on asking, What kind of mnemonic devices were they? Were they like strings tied around the khipukamayuq's finger? Were the knots empty of significance, like the counters of a rosary? Were khipu similar to structural (e.g., architectural) memory-theater-like configurations used in some manner for the recitation of carefully stored bodies of information? Were they like schematic logographic inscriptions? Or, perhaps most *un*likely of all, could they have been syllabic, alphabetic, or other phonologically based notations? Just what kinds of mnemonic devices have scholars considered the khipu to have represented? Unfortunately, we will find that most theorists who have argued that the khipu represented mnemonic devices have been, to say the least, quite vague and unspecific in their definitions of this concept.

Before turning to look at the few explicit arguments characterizing the khipu as a mnemonic recording device, I want to state clearly that although I do not accept the basic tenets of the mnemonic interpretation of the khipu, at least not if it is limited to the memory-theater, string-around-the-finger, or rosary types of mnemonics, I think that memory undoubtedly played an important role in the reading of these devices. As William J Conklin (2002), among others, has pointed out, all script systems represent mnemonic recording devices to one degree or another. Certainly this was true, as we have seen, of the earliest cuneiform economic texts, in which the clay tablets generally recorded only the numbers and nouns of economic transactions; however, in the hands of a knowledgeable Sumerian official, these skeletal texts could be embellished with modifiers and grammatical syntactical elements in the production of a narrative rendering of the transaction in question (see Nissen, Damerow, and Englund 1993: 116–117; and Sampson 1985: 50; on the related issue of the linkage between the logic of writing and the logic of divination in early Mesopotamia, see Manetti 1993: 2–5).

We find a similar situation to that described above in the case of the early texts produced in Linear B. As John Chadwick has noted: ". . . what mattered most to the users of these documents was the numerals. The numbers and quantities are the important details which cannot be confided to the memory; the remainder of the text is simply *a brief note* of what the numerals refer to, headings to enable the reader to identify the person or place associated with the quantity recorded" (1994 [1976]: 27; my emphasis). By reference to the tradition of recording "brief notes" identifying the objects modified by the numerals, we find ourselves again confronting the kind of mnemonics tradition—as in early cuneiform—that connects mnemonics and writing (in the case of Linear B, with syllabic and, to a lesser degree, logographic signs). This prompts us to ask whether or not those who argue that the khipu represented a "mnemonic" recording system would be willing to concede that certain of the string/knot/color combinations could have been accorded logographic values. If not, why not? But if so, then we are thereby at the doorstep of writing by means of the khipu.

Regarding the importance of memory in mnemotechnic and writing systems, I would also note that even in our own alphabetic script, the squiggles that we draw on a piece of paper—the letters of our alphabet—serve to remind us of arrangements of signs denoting groupings of sounds that go together to form the words we wish to indicate (or that have been indicated) in a written text.

On this matter, I would point out that a part of the testimony provided by one of our most interesting and seemingly knowledgeable sources on the khipu, the Peruvian Jesuit mestizo and supposed author of a lost chronicle Blas Valera, seems to confirm that the "reading" of a khipu may, in fact, have been the work of memory alone:

> The tenacity of their memories is noticeably superior to that of Spaniards, even those of outstandingly good memory. The Indians are ingenious in memorizing with the aid of knots, the knuckles and places; and they can moreover use the same knots for various themes and subjects, and when a subject is mentioned they can read off the account as fast as a good reader reads a book, and no Spaniard has yet contrived to do this or to find how it is done. All this springs from the Indians' ingenuity and good memory." (cited in Garcilaso de la Vega 1966: 331)

Before we let the above portion of the testimony of Blas Valera carry the day with regard to the question of whether the khipu was a mnemonic device—at least one of the string-around-the-finger or the memory-theater type—or a writing system, we should note two further points that considerably complicate this picture. First, there is equally explicit testimony from other knowledgeable writers of the colonial period which states that the Inka did, in fact, "write" historical annals and other such discursive types of documents by means of the khipu (see Quilter and Urton 2002), and second, the above comments by Blas Valera are introduced by the following harangue against the Spaniards:

> We moreover are slower in understanding their books than they in following ours; for we have been dealing with them for more than seventy years without ever learning the theory and rules of their knots and accounts, whereas they have very soon picked up not only our writing but also our figures, which is a proof of their great skill. (cited in Garcilaso de la Vega 1966: 331)

Thus, Valera was arguing that even in his own time, the colonizers had remained essentially ignorant of how khipu functioned in record keeping. I think that before the matter is decided with respect to the connection between memory and writing in the khipu on the basis of a part of Blas Valera's testimony, we need to explore more fully—as I intend to do in the present study—what Valera referred to as the "theory and rules of their knots and accounts" (for a study of Blas Valera's ideas about and commentary on khipu, see Hyland 2002).

The Mnemonics Argument in Khipu Studies

A number of scholars who studied the khipu in the past, most notably L. Leland Locke (1912, 1923, 1928), as well as today (e.g., Rappaport and Cummins 1994, 1998), have argued that khipu constituted "mnemonic devices" whose purpose was to aid the khipukamayuq in the recitation of information stored in the memory. We may imagine that we are viewing such a reading in one of the drawings by the late-sixteenth-, early-seventeenth-century native chronicler Felipe Guaman Poma de Ayala (1980 [1615]; see Figure 1.8). The illustration depicts a khipukamayuq, on the right, reporting to the emperor, Topa Ynga Yupanqui, the contents of his khipu (whose information can be seen knotted into the strings of this device), which presumably contains an

1.8. Khipukamayuq of Inka storehouses (Guaman Poma 1980 [1615]: 309 [335]).

accounting of the materials in the state warehouses (*collcas*) shown in the drawing.

Most proponents of the mnemonics interpretation of khipu records have maintained not only that the khipu served as an arrangement of visual and tactile "cues" for the recall of the information retained in the memory of its maker, but also that there were no conventional signs or widely shared translation values assigned to khipu structures that would have allowed one khipukamayuq to read another's khipu or that could have served as a basis for a confirmation of readings among various record keepers throughout the empire. The view characterizing the khipu as based on nonshared, idiosyncratic recording values, or procedures, draws its primary support from the testimony of the mid-seventeenth-century Jesuit chronicler Bernabé Cobo. As Cobo noted:

> In place of writing they used some strands of cord or thin wool strings, like the ones we use to string rosaries; and these strings were called *quipos*. By these recording devices and registers they conserved the memory of their acts, and the Inca's overseers and accountants used them to remember what had been received and consumed. A bunch of these *quipos* served them as a ledger or notebook. . . . There were people designated for this job of accounting. These officials were called *quipo camayos* and the Incas had great confidence in them. These officials learned with great care this way of making records and preserving historical facts. However, not all of the Indians were capable of understanding the *quipos;* only those dedicated to this job could do it; and those who did not study *quipos* failed to understand them. *Even among the quipo camayos themselves, one was unable to understand the registers and recording devices of others. Each one understood the quipos that he made and what the others told him.* (Cobo 1983 [1653]: 253–254; my emphasis)

Since Cobo's testimony is so powerful and seemingly authoritative, especially on the question of the nonstandardized, nonconventional, and nonreciprocally readable nature of the khipu, it is important to mention a couple of conditions regarding his testimony and the times in which he lived that bear on the question of what Cobo may and may not have been aware of. In the first place, Cobo's account was published in 1653, 130 years after the beginning of the Iberian invasion of western South America. Thus, a lot of time had passed since khipu were used openly for official record keeping in day-to-day settings in communities throughout the Andes, much less in Cusco, where Cobo spent most of his time and collected most of his data (Cobo 1983: 100–101). Cusco was the former capital of the Inka Empire and was, by Cobo's time, a heavily Hispanicized city (see MacCormack 2001). However, and more to the point of our concerns here, the khipu had actually been banned, condemned as idolatrous objects, and ordered burned some 70 years before Cobo penned his chronicle! This disposition had occurred as an act of the Third Council of Lima, in 1583 (Urton 1998; Vargas Ugarte 1959). Thus, Cobo himself probably never witnessed khipu being handled, much less read, in circumstances that were *not* fraught with considerable tension or negative, censorious attitudes on the part of Spaniards.

The second point to make with regard to Cobo's testimony is that among those earlier chroniclers—some of whom Cobo used as his sources—who wrote about khipu before the Third Council, during a period when these devices were more commonly seen, used, and produced as sources of historical and legal testimony (e.g., Cieza de León, Sarmiento de Gamboa, Garcilaso de la Vega), none states that khipu could only be read by the person who made them (see Urton n.d.a). For these reasons, I think it is important that we not allow the testimony of this one late chronicler (i.e., Cobo) to be the sole voice establishing for us the parameters of the readability and potentially shared, conventionalized nature of these records.

The situation discussed above regarding the readability of the khipu concerns those records that formed a part of the official documentation of the Inka state, as opposed to any knotted-string records that might have been produced for individual use. This latter point is important, because what is at issue here is not whether or not people were capable of producing private, idiosyncratic record-keeping devices (which they obviously were), but rather, whether or not *state* records that were kept by local, regional, and imperial administrators would or would not have been subject to some requirements of conventionality, transparency, and comparability of recording and reading.

The earliest sustained argument in the modern era for the status of the khipu as a mnemonic device appeared in the work of L. Leland Locke (esp. 1923). Locke compared the khipu to such undoubted mnemonic devices as rosaries and message sticks. From his studies of some forty-two khipu in the American Museum of Natural History, Locke concluded that the khipu was used primarily to sign numbers and that it did not represent a conventional scheme of writing (1923: 31–32; see below). In the course of this study, I show that Locke, in fact, failed to take into account even one-half of the total information encoded in the khipu, and that, therefore, his conclusion to the effect that the "evidence" does not warrant classifying the khipu as a writing system is highly questionable. I address Locke's conclusions on the nature of the khipu record-keeping system in Chapter 7.

The most highly developed form of the mnemonic argument in recent times is in a series of important articles dealing with literacy in the early colonial Andes published by Joanne Rappaport and Tom Cummins (e.g., 1994, 1998). One consistent theme of these scholars' work has been that the introduction of alphabetic literacy into the Andes at the time of the conquest represented a force for significant intellectual, technological, political, and ideological transformation for the native Americans. One reason for this, according to Rappaport and Cummins, was that Andean peoples did not have prior experience with a system of writing—specifically, not with a graphic, alphabetic script (on this subject, see also Quispe-Agnoli 2000). The researchers' primary interest in this series of studies is in exploring the consequences of the Andean confrontation with and consumption of an alphabetic script system and the political—but not economic or numerical (see below)—system that it supported.

In undertaking this critique, I want to stress that I believe that Rappaport and Cummins are completely correct in their analyses of the nature and significance of the transformations wrought by the imposition of alphabetic literacy in the early colonial Andean world. The questions I raise below regarding their work concern what is a relatively minor point for their own arguments and research agenda but one that is of much greater significance for the problems I am concerned with here.

Among Rappaport and Cummins's statements about the nature of khipu mnemonic records, we read the following:

The Andean object which could be said to correspond most closely to the document is the quipu, a mnemonic device of coloured and knotted strings used in Andean cultures to recall various categories of information. . . . The act of writing to communicate presupposes literacy, while mnemonics is based instead on the memorization of facts which are *represented* in an object. The object itself cannot abstractly communicate knowledge as writing does. Rather, it *stands for* categories of knowledge which are then *specified in relation to* memorized data. Thus, the quipu and the quipucamayoc (the one who has memorized the quipu) are not independent of each other in the way that the writer and reader are. (1994: 100; my emphases)

It is clear that Rappaport and Cummins support Cobo's understanding that khipu were not based on shared traditions of signing and meaning, as they state unequivocally that the khipukamayuq and his khipu were inseparable. Beyond that, however, we are confronted in this quotation with precisely the problem I alluded to at the end of the previous section: trying to understand the meaning of any particular representation of "mnemonics," given the varied types of memory techniques and devices that may legitimately be regarded as constituting such systems.

In terms of the concept of something "standing for" something else (see above), we could say, for instance, that a string tied around my finger stands for or "represents" the message I have stored in my memory, but we could also say that, as was true in early cuneiform, a cross inside a circle impressed on a clay tablet represented or stood for the logogram "sheep." Thus, we must ask, What was the nature of the "stand for" or representational relationship between an object in the world (e.g., a census figure, a royal genealogy, a character in a myth) and the knotted-string referent to that object in the khipu that is being proposed in this theory of khipu mnemonics?

The fact is, the concept of something "standing for" something else is extremely complicated. The idea of "standing for" is a central operation around which the great student and philosopher of signs Charles S. Peirce constructed his notion of "sign-action." As Peirce noted, "a sign, or representamen, is something which *stands* to somebody *for* something in some respect or capacity" (cited in Deledalle 2000: 72; my emphases). As the recent commentator on Peircean sign theory Gérard Deledalle notes: "'Stands for' is a perfect definition of the representamen [ca., sign] which 'stands for' something which we do not know yet but that semiosis will possibly indicate in the course of the interpretive process" (2000: 73). Noting that Peirce defined the sign (in one of his many characterizations) as ". . . something by knowing which we know something more" (cited in Johansen 1993: 56), there is clearly, then, a problem with Rappaport and Cummins's characterization of features of khipu as "standing for" something to somebody while maintaining that, in fact, there are no conventionalized sign values incorporated in the khipu—that is, that interpreting these devices is not, after all, a semiotic process. I return at the end of this chapter to the interesting question of how the construction of khipu elements to stand for certain values could have led over time to the development of conventionalized signs. I give a more fulsome discussion of the general nature of khipu signs and sign systems in Chapter 6.

I would also question the meaning of the term "specified" in the above quotation from the work of Rappaport and Cummins. What are the principles of specification that may have been utilized in this mnemonic recording tradition? That is, on what grounds (e.g., hierarchical position? similitude?) might one have specified a connection between any given piece of memorized information and some specific feature(s) of a khipu? We do not find satisfactory answers to such questions in the otherwise very valuable and insightful works by Rappaport and Cummins on Andean literacies.

In regard to the point made earlier about topics involving statistical accounting that have received little attention in the literature by those who have discussed Andean literacies to date, I note that few of these scholars have discussed in any sustained way the numerical records or mathematical accounts concerning censuses, tribute records, and other such matters that are contained in the colonial documentation from the Andes, even though such topics represent the subject matter of a great many—if not the majority—of *all* Andean texts, whether in the khipu or in the written Spanish documents. For instance, in reading Rappaport and Cummins's otherwise thoughtful and insightful studies on literacy in the early colonial Andean world, one is left wondering, for instance, how the khipukamayuq, who spent the better part of every day of their lives studying knotted-string records of numerical accounts, may have thought about the mountains of documents produced by the Spaniards that contained essentially only numbers (i.e., using Hindu-Arabic numerals).

One topic relating to mathematical concerns that could potentially be of great interest and importance for studies of alphabetic literacy and numeracy is whether or not colonial Andean peoples would have developed traditions of viewing the actual numeral signs (1, 2, 3, . . .) as having iconic, symbolic values, as I have described for contemporary Quechua speakers in central Bolivia (Urton 1997: 221–231). The larger point here is that surely the experience of literacy on the part of these former Inka state record keepers would have been significantly different from that of the ordinary Andean villager, who seldom (if ever) attended to the intellectual and technical rigors of recording and carefully studying knotted-string records of numerical (and other?) values.

The issues raised above are emblematic of the absence of general theorizing on the nature of signs in the khipu to date. I return to this matter in Chapter 6, by which time we should be able to begin to lay out certain fundamental principles of a general khipu sign theory.

To conclude this section, in my view, none of the arguments produced to date in support of the mnemonic interpretation of the khipu has specified with thoughtfulness or clarity how the various construction features of these devices might have been used by khipukamayuq as an "aid to the memory." In fact, it is hard to imagine how adherents of the mnemonic interpretive tradition might convincingly theorize concerning khipu mnemonic methods, given the fact that most adherents of this view have supposed that each of these devices was a unique product of the khipukamayuq who made and consulted it.

Scripts and Writing Systems

Defining what constitutes writing is a highly controversial, hotly contested matter (e.g., Boone and Mignolo 1994; Coulmas 1992; Coulmas and Ehlich 1983; Daniels and Bright 1996; DeFrancis 1989; Haas 1976; Harris 1986, 1995; Salomon 2001; Street 1984; Taylor and Olson 1995). Some scholars insist that so-called true writing should be limited to systems based on phonograms, which are the various types and levels of graphemes that denote the sounds of a language. Examples would include alphabetic, syllabic, and (at the margins) logosyllabic script systems. Logosyllabic systems are based on combined logogram plus syllabogram signing units; these include cuneiform and Egyptian and Mayan hieroglyphic writing. I referred to such scripts as "at the margins" of true writing because logograms have conventional semantic but not phonological value; examples would include such signs as 1, 2, 3, whose written forms, as keyed to spoken forms from a few exemplary languages, take the following forms: "one, two, three"; "uno, dos, tres"; or [in Quechua] "uj, iskay, kimsa."

Other students of writing seek to permit a wider range of types of scripts and signing systems—including nonphonologically based ones—within the fold of writing systems (e.g., Boone 1994: 15–17). Such definitions would, for instance, permit musical, dance, and mathematical notation systems, none of which signs phonetic values, to be defined as systems of writing (on such systems, see Aveni 1986; Drake 1986; Goodman 1976; Treitler 1981). Some (e.g., Arnold and Dios Yapita 2000: 46–49) have even suggested that signs such as the designs woven into textiles or scratched or painted onto ceramics should be defined as systems of writing. However, I think such signing devices are best classified as icons bearing conventional but highly abstract, context-specific meanings (see Mitchell 1987). Referring to such productions as writing, while perhaps satisfying what I would argue are essentially politically motivated programs or agendas promoting inclusiveness and multiculturalism (with which I am sympathetic), renders the concept of writing virtually meaningless and (more to the point) useless for analytical purposes.

Elizabeth Boone has argued persuasively that an adequate definition of writing must include provisions for both sound-based ("glottographic") and nonphonological, meaning-based ("semasiographic") sign systems (1994: 15–17; see also Sampson 1985: 29). The definition for writing that she derives on the basis of this relatively (but not absolutely) more inclusive set of considerations is: ". . . the communication of relatively specific ideas in a conventional manner by means of permanent, visible marks." It is unclear to me how nonspecific signs would have to be for them not to conform to Boone's stipulation that the ideas denoted must be "relatively specific." I am in agreement with the definition on this score if we reserve the term for phonological systems as well as those nonphonological glottographic systems based on highly conventionalized sign values (e.g., the logograms known as numeral signs, musical notations, algebraic and other mathematical notations, etc.) but exclude the designs and figures more commonly defined as iconography. On the other hand, since I maintain in this book that the khipu, whose signs were made up of three-dimensional string-and-knot configurations, constituted a system of communication of relatively specific ideas in a conventional manner, I argue that we do not need to retain the restriction in Boone's definition of the signs of writing to "marks"—by which I assume she means graphemes scratched, painted, or otherwise inscribed onto two-dimensional surfaces.

Given the above considerations, I would amend Boone's definition to say that writing is "the communication of specific ideas in a highly conventionalized, standardized manner by means of permanent, visible signs." Having arrived at this revised definition, however, I would also like to subscribe to the qualification that the forms of writing that accomplish the most highly specific level of denotation of ideas are those in which the signs of writing denote the sounds of the language community in question. As I noted earlier, these latter kinds of writing systems are ones that have often been referred to as "true writing." The qualifier is, of course, highly inflammatory and is consistent with the often ethnocentric way in which certain writers have discussed the evolution of (rather than differences between) different types of signing systems (see esp. Gelb 1963: 11–15).

I do not see any solution to this problem other than to drop the label "true writing" and maintain a straightforward distinction between glottographic (both phonologically and nonphonologically based) and semasiographic (non-language-utterance-based) sign systems and then to provide informed commentary on the uses to which various cultures put their respective record-keeping systems. This latter programmatic feature is especially important, because it is clearly the case that some societies have not had a need for complex, phonologically based script systems, and thus they did not invent them, while others did need such systems, so they did invent (or borrow) them. Therefore, the point on which differentiation between different types of signing/recording systems would turn (according to the perspective proposed here) is that of *need,* rather than intelligence.[3]

Finally, I bring this introductory discussion of writing to an end by noting that although I refer at various places to the khipu communication system as a writing system, I use this designation in a generic sense. This is primarily for want of a better term, especially early in my exposition of a signing system in which (as I show later) the sign units signify—or are constituted as—the results of binary decision-making events and string/knot/color manipulations. The knots of khipu may all be assigned strings (i.e., series) of values in binary code. I argue that these coded series were read or interpreted on the basis of conventionalized values that were attached or assigned to particular coded sequences. As we will learn, the nearest analogy to this kind of "writing" is the process of writing binary number (1/0) coded programs for computers. These (computer) coded programs do not themselves constitute "writing"; rather, they provide the strings of electronic information units— e.g., 11100100/ 01000111/ etc.—whereby we can, for instance, type a text on a computer in alphabetic script, as was done with the text the reader is reading at this moment.

I give a complete overview of the theory of binary coding in the khipu at the beginning of Chapter 2. However, I hasten to assure the skeptical reader that khipu were not binary coding devices in some preternatural presaging of a form of technology (the computer) that has entered our own material culture only in the twentieth century. Rather, I show that the khipu was profoundly, legitimately, and of necessity—because it was based on the manipulation of threads in three-dimensional space—based on binary coding.

Representations of Khipu Recording as "Writing"

In contrast to the mnemonic interpretive tradition outlined earlier, many students of the khipu over the years—beginning in the modern era perhaps with Julio C. Tello (1937; cited in Radicati di Primeglio 1964: 17–18)—have argued in favor of an interpretation that sees them more akin to a system of writing (see Arellano 1999; Ascher and Ascher 1997; Conklin 2002; Mignolo 1995: 84–86; Radicati di Primeglio 1964; Sempat Assadourian 2002; Urton 1994, 1998, 2002). Those who have adopted this alternative interpretation generally see the various construction features of the khipu as carrying and conveying what must have been widely shared logical and syntactical properties and semantic values, so that a trained khipukamayuq working in the state bureaucracy could pick up any khipu produced in the state-sanctioned khipu recording tradition and read or interpret the information in that record. The latter would have constituted an integrated system of knowledge, skills, and communicative practices that I believe would qualify, in the eyes of most theorists on writing and literacy, as a writing system (see Harris 1995: 21–32 on "integration" as a fundamental feature of literacy).

Various sources support the notion that the khipu was based on a shared recording tradition. For example, the chronicler Cristóbal de Molina ("el Cuzqueño") says the following with regard to the khipu records:

> . . . they had a very cunning method of counting by strings of wool and knots, the wool being of different colours. They call them quipus, and they are able to understand so much by their means, that they can give an account of all the events that have happened in their land for more than five hundred years. They had expert Indians who were masters in the art of reading the quipus, and the knowledge was handed down from generation to generation, so that the smallest thing was not forgotten. (cited and translated in Locke 1923: 36)

We also have a considerable amount of commentary on the khipu by one of the great Peruvian figures of Spanish-American letters, Garcilaso de la Vega. Garcilaso, a Quechua/Spanish mestizo who was born and raised in Cusco in the mid-sixteenth century and who claimed facility in reading the khipu, suggests that there was some degree of shared record keeping among khipu makers at the local level:

> Although the *quipucamayus* were as accurate and honest as we have said, their number in each village was in proportion to its population, and however small, it had at least four and so upwards to twenty or thirty. *They all kept the same records,* and although one accountant or scribe was all that would have been necessary to keep them, the Incas preferred to have plenty in each village and for each sort of calculation, so as to avoid faults that might occur if there were few, saying that if there were a number of them, they would either all be at fault or none of them. (Garcilaso de la Vega 1966: 331; my emphasis)

The above quotation from Garcilaso is unfortunately not without ambiguity. What can the famed author of the *Comentarios reales* have meant when he asserted that the four to twenty or thirty record keepers in any given village "all kept the same records"? Can we imagine that so many (a minimum of four) khipukamayuq in a village would have invented four—much less thirty!—*different* systems of keeping the *same* records? Such an idea seems to strain one's credulity; surely Garcilaso meant that, however many record keepers there were in a given village, they all kept their own copy/record of the relevant data in what was probably a shared, standardized format, thus giving them the ability to cross-check, double-check, confirm, and contest each others' data and reading.[4] The question that confronts one who adopts the position that the khipu recorded information in some conventionalized manner is: What form might these conventionalized recording units—the khipu signs—have taken? We do not have in the existing literature many serious attempts to address questions such as this.

Perhaps the most sustained effort at theorizing the nature of a possible khipu writing system is in certain works published by Marcia and Robert Ascher (esp. Ascher and Ascher 1997 and M. Ascher 2002). In general terms, I note that the Aschers have stated explicitly that they think the khipu *did,* in fact, constitute a writing system (1997: 78). Their characterization of the recording and information system of the khipu is in the phrase "general recording device"; by this designation, one might suppose that this device *could* have encoded any manner of information, from numbers to word signs (logograms) to, one might even suppose, sound (i.e., language). However, the Aschers have not suggested that the khipu signs contain phonograms, nor do they seem to support such a suggestion (see esp. M. Ascher 2002, R. Ascher 2002, and below). Instead, they argue that the khipukamayuq "used *cues* from a shared informational model within Inca culture, and particularly those aspects of the model related to state affairs" (1997: 78; my emphasis).

The crux of the Aschers' argument is in the distinction between knot values signifying numbers used as *magnitudes* as opposed to knot numbers used as *labels.* The former constituted the basis of recording and accounting in the statistical (quantitative) khipu. As for the notion of the use of khipu number values (in Quechua) as signifying labels, a notion with which I am essentially in agreement, the Aschers suggest this would have taken the form of knot values being used to denote identities, toponyms, titles, and so on. The Aschers have explicitly drawn on number label models from contemporary American society— for example, telephone numbers, Social Security numbers, ISBN numbers, etc. (see esp. M. Ascher 2002)—to provide analogies for how number labels may have been used to sign nonquantitative values (e.g., residence, group identity, status). Perhaps we could say that Garcilaso de la Vega's problematic statement (see Urton 2002) to the effect that the Inka interpreted the knots of their khipu as letters would constitute the nearest testimony I am aware of in support of the Aschers' suggestions.

While the Aschers' thinking and writing on this subject have been quite creative and provocative, we await convincing demonstrations and analyses linking the notion of "number labels" (which is derived from Western approaches to and appropriations of numbers) with recorded Quechua/Inka ideas about and uses of both numbers and labels.[5] This should be an important research agenda for students of Inka and Spanish colonial intellectual history.

In addition to the Aschers' work on khipu writing, in a recent publication (Urton 2002), I have discussed various samples that I refer to as "anomalous" khipu. This designation reflects the fact that these samples have knot types and placements that violate the basic recording techniques and structural principles of decimal number registry followed in the majority of khipu. I have hypothesized that these khipu signed nonquantitative—"label"-like—narrative values, perhaps in the form of logograph-like signifying units. I refer to this study at appropriate points throughout the present work.

On the matter of the possibility that khipu *could* (not *did*) contain phonograms, I will also state here that I see no reason to argue that the makers and users of the khipu *could not* have attributed whatever values they chose, including phonetic, to any given feature of the khipu. Whether they actually *did* that or not for *any* given sign value—ideographic, logographic, phonetic—other than numerical values (which we know they did record) remains to be determined.

Finally, we also have the very interesting but highly problematic material relating to a supposed khipu "syllabic writing" system in a number of books and articles that generally fall under the rubric of "the Naples document" (e.g., see Adorno 1998; Animato, Rossi, and Miccinelli 1989; Cantù 2001; Domenici and Domenici 1996; Laurencich Minelli 1996, 1999a, 1999b, 2001; Ossio 2000). The gist of the argument here is that there may have existed a system of syllabic writing by means of the khipu that was linked to a set, or class, of these devices that contained iconographic symbols tied into the strings. The documents attesting to such a system make many other startling claims about the life histories of certain important people in early colonial Peruvian history (esp. Blas Valera and Guaman Poma de Ayala).

The problem with this documentary material is that scholars have not been allowed free access to study the documents, and people pursuing khipu research remain deeply divided over the authenticity and (*if* they are not authentic early colonial documents) the date of the possible forgery of the documents implicated in this ongoing controversy. In my own view, the evidence strongly supports the notion that the supposed Inka syllabic writing system described in these documents was probably a mid-to late-seventeenth-century fabrication or invention—produced out of complicated political motives—that was made by some party or parties interested in promoting positive, politically motivated representations of Inka intellectual accomplishments (cf. Cañizares-Esguerra 2001: 114–120, and Hyland 2002).

The Hypothetical Conventionalization of Signs in "Khipu Writing"

Before turning in Chapter 2 to the new theory for khipu binary coding that I put forward and elaborate in this book, I want to return for a moment to consider the notion—which I am developing somewhat further than the original suggestion by Rappaport and Cummins (see above)—that khipu operated by way of structures, images, or some other manner of constructed entities to "stand for" objects or values that the khipukamayuq wanted to remember. This seems to me, in general terms, to be an interesting notion but one that deserves more extended analysis than it is given in the article cited above. For instance, how might such a relationship work itself out—specifically, how might this process be repeated in practice—over time? And how, in its reproduction over time, might such a process have led to a conventionalization of signs in a (hypothetical) khipu signing system?

Let us say, for instance, that a khipukamayuq made a certain string configuration—a specific combination of spinning, plying, knotting, and dyeing strings—and assigned it the value of (or made it "stand for") a certain place-name, or age grade, or mythological event. When the record keeper *next* wanted to indicate (construct a "memory cue" for) that *same* object, value, or event, is it not likely that, rather than assigning it to a completely novel string configuration, he would have constructed the same (old) configuration and assigned to it the (now) familiar value? Would not this configuration then gradually over time take on the "conventional" value of this particular place-name, age grade, or mythological event, at least for the khipukamayuq in question? Furthermore, as the numerous record keepers in a given community interacted with each other, is it not reasonable to suppose that they would have seen it in their collective interest to rely on the same or similar string configurations to sign—that is, to "stand for"—the same values, objects, and events, thus leading over time to a conventionalization of signs among the community of record keepers?

The above scenario seems no more nor less reasonable than to suppose that people who continuously interacted with each other would over time adopt the same sequences of sounds as the conventional "names" of things. That is, the notion of record keepers adopting conventionalized signs in keeping records seems consistent with the people of that same community adopting and sharing conventional linguistic signs; the latter is a process we are certain occurred to some degree in the context we are discussing, since Quechua, the language of administration in the Inka Empire, was spread broadly along the spine of the Andes, from Ecuador southward through Bolivia and Chile. My point here is to suggest that to think that the khipu record keepers might have invented whole new configurations of string structures every time they set about constructing khipu accounts for well-known objects, recurring events, and communally sanctioned values seems to me to impute a level of exoticized arbitrariness to their actions that makes no sense, at least not to me. Thus, it is theoretically possible that khipu structures may indeed have been constructed to "stand for" certain objects or values and that, over time, these structures would have become the conventionalized signs for these particular values or objects in a system of khipu "writing."

The above may be the conditions that may have led to the emergence and standardization of a system of writing. Such a khipu-based system in the Andes may or may not have been phonologically based, a quality that some (e.g., DeFrancis 1989) but by no means all (e.g., Boone and Mignolo 1994) students of literacy and writing ascribe as an essential characteristic of "true" writing. Whether "khipu writing" was, at some yet-to-be-determined level, linked to phonological signs neither

I nor (I believe) anyone else working in this area today can say, since no one today has ever seen or heard an Inka khipukamayuq read and interpret a khipu. But whether it was phonologically based or not, the system would have clearly been based on a body of conventional "signs" (i.e., string/knot/color/material configurations) denoting standardized values that would have been known to those who were educated in, or initiated into, the time-honored system of signing.

Overview of the Organization of the Book

I begin Chapter 2 by laying out in an extended manner the theory of binary coding that I am advancing in this work. I also give an accounting of the museum studies of khipu carried out by various scholars (including myself) over the years, as well as describe methods that have been used in the study of these remarkable objects.

In Chapter 3, I begin explicating the theory of binary coding in the khipu by examining several features of these devices that are produced by the physical processing or manipulation of raw materials. This begins with the selection of materials for construction, followed by the spinning and plying of the raw material to produce strings, and then the dyeing of the strings. The strings are then attached to what is known as the primary cord, and finally the strings are knotted. I show that each of these operations is a result of decision making and string manipulation in a binary mode.

In Chapter 4, we turn to certain symbolic components of the khipu binary coding system. These include numbers (of particular importance is the significance of the odd/even relationship in Quechua numeration) as well as colors. In the section on numbers, we shall also discuss the nature of, and the relationship between, numerical and non-numerical ("anomalous") khipu. As for colors, we will see that, although they were conceived of within an overall binary framework, a significant modification and expansion of coding units was required in order to sign this component of the khipu information system.

Chapter 5 focuses on two issues resulting from the detailed information on binary coding presented in Chapters 3 and 4. These issues are, first, the amount of information—the potential number of signing units—that could have been signed by means of the khipu binary codes; and second, proposing a hypothesis for the procedures that may have been followed in decoding the information in certain of the binary-coded khipu. The latter involves translating khipu binary fabric structures into arrays of contrastively colored (e.g., black and white) stones.

With the theory articulated and the data presented on binary coding in previous chapters, in Chapter 6 I take up the general questions: What was the nature of khipu signs? How were signs combined and interrelated in the production of a larger sign system? Addressing these questions will require that we consider theoretical and comparative literature from various fields of study concerning sign theory, the theory of markedness in linguistic systems, and the poetic device known as parallelism. Drawing on these diverse descriptive and theoretical approaches to signing, versification, and narrativity, we are able to articulate a general theory for how khipukamayuq might have organized linked, hierarchically related semantic couplets in the recording of information in the binary khipu code.

In the concluding chapter, we will return for a few final words concerning the question with which we began this work: What kind of recording system did the khipu represent? Was this a mnemonic recording device? A writing system? Or do we need some new, perhaps hybrid designation for the type of records and record-keeping practices carried on by the Inka khipukamayuq in their manipulation of strings in a remarkably complex system of binary coding?

CHAPTER **2**

Theory and Methods in the Study of Khipu Binary Coding

In this study, I propose to address the questions of Inka recording and writing by putting forth a new theory on the methods that I believe may have been used to encode and decode (or read) information in these devices. The procedure that I use for presenting and elaborating this theory takes the form of a systematic and comprehensive accounting of the various construction techniques involved in the fabrication of khipu. Because of its careful attention to the description of form and variability in these textile fabrications, the theory developed herein has the virtue that if the general and admittedly more daring ideas regarding Inka "writing" contained in this work do not bear up to the intense scrutiny to which I hope they will be subjected in the future, we will nonetheless at least have made a significant descriptive and methodological advance in the study of khipu by virtue of the considerable amount of specific and, in many cases, new information and observations on these objects that I offer in the course of this study. Let us turn below to the essential problem: How could one "write" using strings, knots, and colors, rather than pen, paper, and graphemes?

The central argument I make in the remainder of this book, stated in just a few words, is that the physical features resulting from the manipulation of fibers in the construction of khipu constituted binary-coded sequences; these coded sequences—each represented by a spun, plied, dyed, and carefully crafted knot (see Figure 2.1)—were the sites of the storage of the units of information in a (hypothetical) shared system of binary record keeping among khipu keepers and readers throughout the Inka Empire.[1]

With regard to the general issue of systems of coding information, I remind the reader that I began the previous chapter by talking about

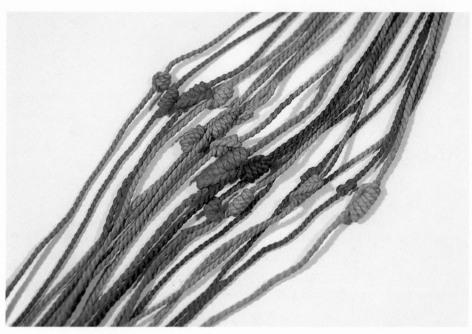

2.1. Knots on a cotton khipu (Museum für Völkerkunde, Berlin, no number).

computers and binary coding. I did so because I believe that a consideration of computer information technology, and in particular a careful thinking through of the nature of the "interface" between a code and the script(s) that it encodes, may provide a useful model for conceptualizing what I hypothesize to have been the relationship between the storing of information and the reading of messages in the khipu. I suggest that this relationship may be likened to that between the signs of a binary code, on the one hand, and the message—usually in the form of some recognizable, "readable" script—transmitted by means of that binary code, on the other hand. I elaborate on this paradigm below.

In the technology of communicating by means of, for instance, e-mail, we work on a keyboard that allows us to produce on the computer monitor in front of us a typewritten version of a message. The message that we perceive on the screen before us in a familiar script (e.g., Spanish, Japanese, English) exists inside the computer in the form of binary-coded sequences in which each mark (e.g., alphabetical letter, comma, hyphen, etc.) that is produced by touching a key on the keyboard coincides with, or is carried by, a particular eight-binary-digit (ab-

breviated as "bit") sequence of 1s and 0s. These eight-bit sequences have
arbitrarily been assigned to the characters in the system known as the
ASCII (American Standard Code for Information Interchange) code.
The use of eight bits of coded information is, within certain limits, arbitrary; that is, computer systems would work adequately if the origi-
nators of the system had decided to use, for instance, seven- or nine-bit
sequences. It is also relevant to point out in regard to the relative arbitrariness of eight-bit sequences as the foundation of modern computing
technology that early computers relied on decimal- rather than binary-
coded information (Eck 1995: 6). One point to stress is that to propose a theory of binary coding in the Inka khipu is not to "jump on the
bandwagon" of today's preoccupation with computers and computing;
rather, it is to insist that whereas computers came to adopt binary coding
through a process of trial and error, khipu were, for the most part, binary coding devices *by nature*. I will return to this point shortly.

As for how binary coding "interfaces" with scripts in computers, each
word that we see in script on our computer screen coincides with a
series of eight-bit sequences within the electronically stored information inside the computer. For example, a word typed on our keyboard
as "cat" corresponds to the binary code: 01000011 [= c] 01100001
[= a] 01110100 [= t] (Eck 1995: 7; see also Scott 1985: 10–16; Wilks
et al. 1996). When instructed to send the e-mail message, the computer
transmits the binary number sequences as electronic signals—that is, as
patterned arrangements of 1s and 0s (or on/off, positive/negative electronic signals). The computer sends the binary-coded message to another computer, which receives the electronic code. The receiving computer translates the binary-coded message back into the same script seen
in the original message.

Now, no one would confuse a string of 1s and 0s for (for instance) a
text written in English by means of the twenty-six letters of the alphabet, plus the number signs and perhaps a few other signs and symbols
(e.g., : <). Nonetheless, it is a conventionalized arrangement of 1s and
0s of the binary number coding system (i.e., the ASCII code) that makes
it possible for us to communicate e-mail messages in (as in the example
given here) an alphabetic script. I argue in this book that the systems of
patterned differences in spinning, plying, knotting, numbers, and colors
in the khipu are *all* binary in nature. These various components of the

khipu recording system interact with each other to constitute what we may call the ASCII of the khipu information system.

Concerning the character of these coded pieces of information, I show that the Inka and other khipu users of the ancient Andes relied on seven-bit sequences, rather than the (arbitrarily chosen) eight-bit sequences of the ASCII system. I suggest that these seven-bit sequences were sometimes (though by no means always) displayed for reading in the form of stones that were arrayed in patterned sequences—seven-bit linear arrays of, for instance, black stones and white stones. Note, however, that the khipu constructions and the arrays of stones represented two versions of the code, not the script, of messages in the khipu information system. In order actually to read a message in the khipu, we need something like a table, or a "code book," that gives the translation values for the particular binary-coded sequences for each unit of information encoded into a khipu. As yet, we do not have such a table or book for translating these seven-bit sequences into intelligible, interpretable messages. What I define herein, then, are simply the binary structures, or patterned systems of differences, in khipu construction features into and out of which khipu messages were encoded and decoded as they passed from sender to receiver and back again in Inka administrative interactions. Before moving on, I would point out the fascinating comparative case, discussed by John DeFrancis, that sending telegrams in China is done by converting the almost 10,000 characters of Mandarin into a four-digit code: "Thus the five characters used to write *míngtian zhongwu dáo* 'arriving tomorrow noon' would be sent as 2494 1131 0022 0582 0451. The dispatching and receiving clerks have available a code book listing the characters and their numerical codes" (DeFrancis 1989: 238). This situation is roughly analogous to the one I am hypothesizing for khipu signing by means of binary coding.

The perceptive reader will recognize a potential problem, or at least an odd quandary, presented by the theoretical orientation on the nature of the khipu information and communication system outlined above: Why, when all other ancient civilizations that developed writing systems did so by straightforwardly inventing and innovating on the scripts for those systems, with graphemes variously representing syllabic, logographic, logosyllabic, and other two-dimensional inscribed units of information, did the Inka develop not a script but rather a medium (the khipu) for registering binary "codes for scripts"? That is, why didn't the Inka just invent an iconic, grapheme-based system of signing information?

I think the most satisfactory explanation for the question raised above relates to the status and physical characteristics of the medium—cloth—of which the khipu represented one form, or expression. In a seminal article published forty years ago, John V. Murra (1962) instructed us on the central role of cloth as a marker of status, wealth, power, and authority in Inka statecraft. Clearly, cloth was not just any medium among the Inka; it was the medium of choice, and as such, the records of state were, not surprisingly, fabricated of this material. As for the physical characteristics of this medium as they are "inscribed" into the three-dimensional textile constructions, the khipu recorded information (at least partially) in a binary manner, choosing one *or* the other of two possibilities—in the movement of strings right *or* left, over *or* under, and to the front *or* to the back of other strings.

Thus, the system we're considering here should not be conceived of as *non*-graphic and *non*-two-dimensional, as though the khipu can or should be defined by what it is *not;* rather, the khipu was (positively) three-dimensional and tactile. Furthermore, most of the operations whereby khipu were constructed were, by virtue of the procedures of moving strings through three-dimensional space, inherently *binary* (i.e., based on the selection of one or the other of two possible, opposed states) in nature. One task that I confront later in this study is to show that numbers and colors—the two principal linguistic, symbolic components of the khipu information system—were conceptualized and organized in the khipu records in ways that integrated them into the binary recording procedures outlined above.

In sum, in place of inscribed graphemes, and in conformity with the three-dimensional nature of the high status and abundantly available medium they selected for record keeping, the Inka developed a system of visual and tactile string structures that communicated particular bodies of information—for example, statistical (census data), narrative (myths and genealogical records), and other genres of texts—*in a binary code.*[2] To return briefly to the analogy with computers articulated earlier, it is as though all other ancient civilizations developed graphic scripts in forms similar to the images seen on our computer monitors, whereas the

Inka devised a system more closely resembling the binary digital coding sequences of the ASCII code: out of view, inside the workings of the computer.

Mary Frame has provided an intriguing analog for the system of binary coding that I have outlined above. In her analysis of the elaborate woven tapestry designs—called *tukapu*—that adorn many Inka royal tunics (*unku*), Frame makes the following observations and suggestions:

> Just as *quipu* cords can combine even or odd numbers at each plying stage, the *t'oqapu* contain number attributes ranging up to nine, and some multiples beyond, through spatial divisions. Inversions in color, value, and direction suggest that meaning in *t'oqapu* is often couched in binary oppositions, a basic principle in fabric structure imagery. (2001: 135)

Thus, perhaps the refocusing of the analysis of khipu around binary coding, which I argue for herein, will have the added benefit of helping us to identify a connection between khipu and *tukapu*—a long-standing (and so far frustrated) objective of Inka studies.

I maintain that the construction of any given khipu was realized in the process of moving through seven frames, or levels of decision making, in producing each site of information in a khipu; each knot on a khipu constituted a fully constructed "site of information." A spun, plied, dyed, but unknotted pendant string represented a partial inscription. The final "message" conveyed by any given seven-bit sequence was the khipukamayuq's reading of the interconnected set of decisions that had been made (either by himself or by another member of the administrative hierarchy) regarding each of the seven levels of binary decision making to be outlined below.

As for the question of how readings were performed, I cannot answer this question entirely satisfactorily at the present time. In general terms, I think that many khipu may have been read "directly," as it were, by the khipukamayuq studying the spun, plied, dyed knots and rendering their standardized meanings or sense according to some conventional knot unit values or formulae. I speculate later on the possible character and organizational features of such translations. I also argue that, in some cases, readings were performed by creating a display on the ground of information recorded in the khipu in the form of arrays of

stones. In some instances, these manipulations may have constituted calculations on quantitative values recorded on the reference khipu (Platt
2002; Urton 1998). In other settings, such arrays may have taken the
form of arrangements of contrastively colored (e.g., black and white)
stones that the khipukamayuq interpreted in the production of some
manner of narrative, ritualistic (e.g., poetic) rendering in a public or
ceremonial setting. The practice of "interfacing" arrays of stones in reading khipu accounts is well attested in the historical literature (Bertonio
1984 [1612]; Platt 1987: 82–87; Urton 1997: 191–194, 1998; and
see below). The stones would have been laid out as a record of the sequence of binary decision-making events that had been carried out in
the production of each completed sign unit (i.e., knot) in the binary-
coded khipu. A hypothetical array, or binary sequence, of white and
black stones might appear as follows: ○○●○●●○. This sequence, representing the binary-coded information of just one knot on a single
khipu, can be likened to an (attenuated) ASCII sequence: 0010110.

Inka "Insistence"

Anyone who has any familiarity with research on the khipu and who
read one of the phrases mentioned earlier, "code of the khipu," will have
been reminded of the seminal work on the khipu, entitled *Code of the
Quipu*, which was first published by Marcia and Robert Ascher in 1981
(Ascher and Ascher 1997; see also 1969, 1975, 1978; and M. Ascher
1986, 1991). The reader who made this connection will also have wondered, particularly if he/she has actually read the Aschers' groundbreak-
ing study, what can possibly be added to our understanding of the
code of the khipu beyond what the Aschers articulated so clearly in
their analysis in their original study and in subsequent publications. The
answer is that while the Aschers have instructed us with considerable
clarity on the significance of numbers (primarily when used as quantities), as well as on the spacing or grouping of strings and the patterning
of colors in the khipu, they did not report data pertaining to the actual
construction of khipu, such as observations on the directions of spinning, plying, and knotting of strings, the variations in attachment of
strings to primary cords, or information pertaining to what we could
call the cultural meanings of colors and numbers in Quechua, the language of Inka administration. It will be in these terms that I believe we

can add further insights into the code(s) of the khipu that will take us beyond those articulated by the Aschers in their foundational study of these remarkable recording devices.

In order to begin to address the questions raised in this and the preceding chapter, I want to recall what was perhaps the central methodological and theoretical point stressed by the Aschers in *Code of the Quipu*. In Chapter 3 of that work, entitled "Inca Insistence," the Aschers articulated the idea—taken from Gertrude Stein's famous remark "a rose is a rose is a rose is a rose"—of cultural "insistence," which is the process whereby, on a day-to-day basis and in all domains of its material life, a civilization defines its essential character through the pervasive and repetitious rehearsal or reproduction of its core values and ways of doing and organizing things. We might say that, as the Aschers deploy this concept, insistence is equivalent to the combination of what we are otherwise familiar with in anthropological theory as structuralism and the concept of the *habitus* as it was developed in the practice theory of Pierre Bourdieu (1979; see also de Certeau 1984), or in the concept of "structuration" as articulated by Anthony Giddens (1983). As the Aschers stated the matter, ". . . insistence is pervasive; it appears in the small as well as in the large. [T]he facility to identify it increases with knowledge of the whole. . . . Furthermore, every time it is successfully identified from a detail, the concept itself passes a test" (1997: 39).

The aspect or expression of Inka insistence—or practice and reproduction of structures—that emerges in the course of the detailed study that we undertake here of structures and relations among variable and patterned elements in the khipu is the repetition of, or the insistence on, what I refer to herein as "binary coding."

The reader might well ask at this point: How does the pervasiveness of binary coding in the khipu constitute an expression of insistence? That is, in what way(s) does the grounding of the principal Inka record-keeping device in repetitive procedures of selecting between one or the other of a pair of options in binary opposition to each other represent a form of continuity with other similar procedures and forms of organization in Inka society and culture? The answer, discussed more thoroughly in Chapter 6 but important to state here in a general form, is that khipu were constructed with these particular kinds of binary operations as the means of recording information in a society that was typified to an extraordinary degree by dual organization—for instance, in its moiety systems as well as in other organizational and symbolic forms (Urton 1990; Zuidema 1964, 1982).

I hasten to stress that what I am arguing here is *not* that there was a kind of profound mentalist, or psychological, force of dualism underlying and determining all Inka structures and practices; rather, my claim is more modest and, one could say, instrumental. That is, I note first that in Andean (and most other) moiety systems, every individual in a community belongs to one *or* the other of the pair of opposed social categories (moieties); however, *both* categories must always be present. Binary opposition does not mean the elimination of one in favor of the other, but rather, the selection between one or the other of two ever present pairs; this was true of Inka moiety organization as well as of binary coding in the khipu. Without denying the inherently binary nature of many khipu string construction and manipulation operations, nonetheless, I also want to insist that, as instruments for recording information pertaining to dual and binary sociopolitical systems, the recording units and information system of the khipu were themselves reflective of, and built up around, dual and binary values, relations, and symbolic features. Thus, khipu were dual and binary in relation to their representative, reportative, and information-storage objectives and functions *because* they existed within a society organized in a dualistic manner, not because the khipukamayuq were incapable of thinking or acting in other modes or registers. I will return to this topic in Chapter 6.

Markedness Theory in Binary Coding

It may be informative and helpful to the reader for me to anticipate at this point the central interpretive problem that will arise in the course of this study as we proceed with the exposition of the system of binary coding in the khipu. The problem I am referring to emerges from the imperative—which increases over the course of the observations and analyses presented in the following two chapters—to explain what types of content could have been signed by means of the relentless construction of binary coding signs utilized in the khipu information system (Figure 2.2).

The hypothesis that I propose and attempt to support, especially in Chapter 6, is that the best place to turn for a theory responding to the above question is to what is known in linguistics as "markedness" theory. This theory was developed most extensively and cogently in the

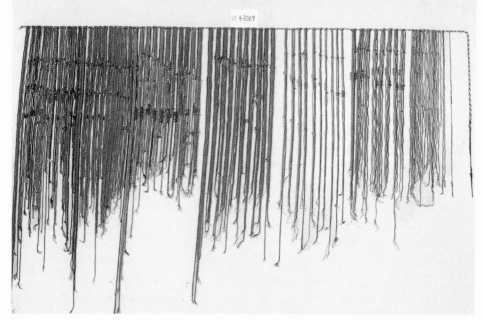

2.2. Large cotton khipu (Museum für Völkerkunde, Berlin, VA 47069).

works of Roman Jakobson (1960, 1966; see Caton 1987). Markedness refers to relationships between pairs of items, often in adjacent lines of poetry, that are usually complementary or opposed to each other in a relationship of binary opposition (Utaker 1874; Waugh 1982). In his studies, Jakobson found, for instance, that poetic forms often construct their vivid imagery, metric versification, and content of meaning by means of weighted (hierarchically related) pairs of terms. One member of these pairs (the "unmarked" term), which we might say represents the default value of the two terms, carries significance at a general level; the other member of the pair (the "marked" term) is the more narrowly defined term, denoting the (or a) special case or a more precisely specified domain of meaning. The marked term, or value, is often portrayed as being inside of, or subordinate to, the unmarked value (Andrews 1990: 9–13; Waugh 1982: 302–303). The unmarked category or term is also often understood to be the term that does not contain (or "neutralizes") the special designation that defines the particular character of the marked term; it is the possession of some distinctive feature that sets the marked term off as a special case (Tomic 1989).

An example of an unmarked/marked (respectively) binary set of terms is the pair man/woman. In many semantic systems (and this was true of American English until quite recently), one might use the un-marked term (man) in constructing a generic statement such as, "all mankind is one." In this phrase, the sentiment expressed is commonly assumed to apply to both men and women. However, if one were to use the *marked* member of this oppositional pair and say, "all woman-kind is one," this would generally be understood to be an expression of some quality or characteristic of women alone—that is, the statement would not be assumed to apply to both women *and* men. Such for-mulations, which are culturally and historically situated, can obviously become contested under conditions of social, political, and ideological change and transformation, as in the example discussed here (see Waugh 1982: 305).

I would also note that Joseph Greenberg has argued (1966; Batti-stella 1996: 14–15) that *frequency* may be a significant measure of markedness; that is, according to Greenberg, the unmarked category would appear more frequently than the marked. Ferenc Kiefer argues the related notion that the unmarked member of a pair has a greater range of applicability, that is, ". . . the range of applicability decreases with the increase of markedness," though he sees this as a consequence of markedness, rather than as one of its essential properties (1989: 122).

Bruce Mannheim in particular has introduced markedness theory, and the related concept of parallelism, into the field of Andean studies (1998). This has principally taken the form of studies of "semantic cou-plets" (a term Mannheim prefers to "parallelism") in Quechua poetry and *waynus* (folk/country songs of the Andes). I discuss Mannheim's work on markedness and parallelism in Chapter 6, where I suggest that khipu coding may have constituted a system for recording binary—marked/unmarked—categories in Inka canonical literature. This could have been accomplished either by assigning a marked/unmarked pair to a particular knot configuration or by assigning a marked semantic value to one binary-coded knot and a linked, unmarked value to its neighbor.

For the moment, the important thing to keep in mind as we pro-ceed through the succeeding chapters is this: When we find (as we will) that the khipu information system was grounded in construction pro-cedures based on choosing one or the other of pairs of binary expres-sions or structural features, we must ask whether or not the choices that

were made—as represented in the physical features of khipu samples—
might have represented selections between, or pairings of, marked and
unmarked morphological or semantic elements in Quechua/Inka poetry
or other ritual, canonical narrative forms. Pursuing such an interpretive strategy, which I expand on in Chapter 6, could provide us with a
potentially powerful strategy and paradigm for charting out construction patterns and relations between elements in the khipu binary coding
system that may have been used to sign certain syntactical structures and
semantic values in Inka recorded traditions.

What Did the Khipu Signs Denote?

The approach to the interpretation of the khipu sign system laid out in
this and the previous chapter, and in particular my supposition that binary coding could even have constituted a system for denoting language
utterances (whether phonological or not [e.g., logograms]), needs some
amplification and clarification, especially in regard to two recently published articles, one by Tristan Platt (2002), the other by Frank Salomon
(2002). Before addressing the concerns raised by these authors, I want
to make clear that the works in question are important and valuable contributions to the khipu literature—after all, these two articles are in a
volume I co-edited (Quilter and Urton 2002). My quibble is not with
their respective analyses of the data that are primarily under investigation in the two articles, but rather with their inferences about the relevance of those data and analyses for *Inka* (i.e., pre-Columbian) record-
keeping practices, which is the focus of my concern here.

Tristan Platt's study addresses the fascinating history of the interaction and contest between Spanish written documents and native Aymara knotted-string accounts (called *chino* in Aymara) in court cases
involving tribute payments by the Sacaca Indians of central Bolivia to
their *encomendero* in the 1580s. In the course of this article, and in re-
sponse to suggestions I made in an earlier article concerning the standardization of recording elements and signing conventions in the Inka
khipu (see Urton 1994), Platt notes:

> This [i.e., my own conclusion] implies that all khipu were transpar-
> ently intelligible to all state bureaucrats, ignoring clear suggestions
> by Cobo, Capoche, and Murúa that many khipu, like local dialects (or
> perhaps—following Murúa—even languages), contained local de-

sign features that would naturally have appeared "impenetrable" to strangers from a different regional tradition of communication and khipu construction. (2002: 231)

Platt is undoubtedly right that there were differences in record keeping throughout the empire. Nonetheless, my point then and now is that *if* the Inka Empire was a state (as most scholars of Andean civilizations accept that it was), then it would have been an objective of state record keepers to encourage, if not insist on, standardization around procedures that they (the state administrators) would have sanctioned and attempted to control. This would have been, as is true always and everywhere, contested at the local level, yet that does not belie the state's interest in creating and trying to insist on standardized procedures (on this general point, see the fascinating article on state insistence on "legible" surnames in Scott, Tehranian, and Mathias 2002). The U.S. Internal Revenue Service will not be happy if, on April 15, I submit my own version and understanding of my obligatory taxation accounting to the state in whatever format I wish to submit it!

Finally, Platt adduces testimony concerning the nature of khipu records from three colonial sources—Capoche [1585], Cobo [1653], and Murúa [1590]—all of whom wrote *after* khipu had been officially abolished and declared idolatrous objects by the Third Council of Lima in 1583 (Vargas Ugarte 1959). I am not convinced that such testimony can have accurately characterized the intent of Inka state record keepers from 50–125 years earlier, during the pre-Hispanic era. Saying this, I certainly agree with Platt's general point that it is always the case that people in local communities—particularly when state imposition is accompanied by attempts to change local linguistic habits, religious customs, and ethnic composition—will struggle to create as much space and autonomy for themselves as possible.

Salomon's study is an exceptionally important analysis of a set of ten khipu from the central highland Peruvian community of Tupicocha. These samples date from sometime during the period from the mid–seventeenth century to the early twentieth century C.E. (Salomon 2002: 301). The ten khipu are distributed, as ancestral patrimony, among the ten *ayllu* (sociopolitical and communal labor groups) of the community. The *ayllu* members (*socios*) lavish great care and attention on these khipu, combing them out, wearing them *bandolero*-style in certain community festival events, and storing them away in the house of their keepers. The Tupicochans do not claim the ability to "read" or interpret these khipu, nor do they permit alterations to be made in them.

Salomon argues that certain construction features of the Tupicochan khipu suggest that pendant strings may have been more movable in the past, and that the community and *ayllu* officials who kept these records (probably for organizing communal labor events) shuffled the strings along the main cords in accordance with shifting work regimes, changing patterns of community obligations, or altered politico-ritual agendas (Salomon 2002: 310). Salomon maintains, in the end, that the Tupicochan khipu—though he generalizes this conclusion to Inka khipu as well (p. 310)—were not record-keeping devices; rather, he states, they were operational devices, or "simulators for working toward social rationality" (p. 310). In his general conclusion, Salomon states:

> The basic structures of these khipu . . . were in my view not intended as archival records but as simulation tools or "game boards," cycled over and over, handed on to successive officeholders, and presumably "rewritten" in successive uses. As for the data cords, perhaps a closer simile would be a deck, as of cards. Pendants may have represented a finite set of categorized entities, such as male/female/underage/ overage workers, which had to be distributed among a planned set of occasions, such as collective work days keyed to the irrigation cycle. The users of the artifact, probably the ayllu members in meetings coordinated by officers, would have "played" the deck, deploying it so as to bring out a workable pattern for the leaders to administer. Much of the intellectual effort of modern ayllu and community affairs concerns deploying the "deck" of available resources in just such a way. The khipu medium is well suited to the task. (Salomon 2002: 314)

Let me begin to address the perspective introduced here by saying that I find myself in sympathy, certainly in philosophical and aesthetic terms, with these conclusions, and have myself concluded a recent article on the collection of khipu from Chachapoyas in a similar spirit (Urton 2001). This interpretation is in line with the very best postmodern literary critical rethinking of the nature of texts and their (potential) multiple readings, as well as it is cognizant of the problem of authoritative versus more highly politically, culturally, and individually nuanced uses and appropriations of texts, whether oral or written.

However, it seems to me that we are thrown back to the same kinds of issues that I addressed earlier in commenting on Platt's article concerning the Sacaca *chino*. For one thing, having myself lived for several years in farming communities—one in particular (Pacariqtambo) that was organized by a complex system of *ayllu* and moieties (Urton 1990)—and having participated as a worker at various tasks in numerous communal work parties, I am familiar with the kinds of public *ayllu* record-keeping practices (in written form) that Salomon has described from his fieldwork in Tupicocha. One thing that has been abundantly clear to me is that "freeloaderism" (i.e., letting your mates do your job, if you can get by with it) is a highly developed art, and *ayllu* officials must constantly check and recheck their *ayllu* rolls to be sure their mates have performed their service duties (which generally give one access to communal lands and other goods). In my view, too much "shuffling of the deck" of *ayllu* records, without a clear accounting of who actually worked and when, will result in a good proportion of the group simply disappearing—in other words, going back to their own fields and doing their own personal work (e.g., see my description of the problems of coordinating and organizing local labor service as experienced by provincial authorities and NGO officials in Pacariqtambo in the mid-1980s; Urton 1992: 235–240).

Certainly the Spaniards who tried to nail down accurate census figures in the early colonial period were aware that large numbers of people eluded them, heading up into the mountains just before the census takers arrived (Stern 1986: 103, 127). I also believe that were it not for certain important forms of largesse and surveillance procedures that were maintained by the Inka state—such as state reciprocity to *mit'a* laborers, placing local *curaca* officials in charge of supervising the performance of state business, and a hierarchy of record keepers inside and outside the local community—the Inka themselves would have faced similar problems of compliance. Though I am certain local-level officials would have wanted to keep local accounts to oversee the distribution of labor service (the form in which tribute was levied in the empire), I believe they would have had to account for the performance of that service to outside officials; in the absence of such accounting outside the village, I do not see how the state could have functioned or reproduced itself. That is, in the absence of a system of checks and balances on state resources, I don't see how we could maintain that the Inka polity was indeed a state.

Garcilaso de la Vega actually gives quite explicit testimony on this matter when he states that the Inka governors of the provinces were shown the contents of storehouses in each village and that "the Inca governor of each province was required by law to keep a copy of the [khipu] accounts in his possession so that no deception could be practiced by either the Indian tribute payers or the official collector" (1966: 275). It would not have made much sense if the governors kept copies of these accounts—guarding against fraud—but were unable to interpret or read them!

Finally, as for Salomon's point about certain construction features of the Tupicochan khipu that suggest to him that these devices may have been retied and elements moved around with some frequency, I would say the following. Having studied closely some 450 archaeological samples of khipu, I have indeed seen some evidence, though not a great deal, for the kinds of textual "rewriting" operations that Salomon believes may have characterized Tupicochan khipu manipulation practices (e.g., untying knots, shuffling strings along the main cord, tying pairs of strings together). However, in the absence of more convincing evidence from samples of pre-Columbian khipu, or from documentary accounts suggesting that these records were altered in this manner, I remain unconvinced that this view of flexible, continuously rewritten texts finds even a modest level of evidentiary support.

While I think the studies by Platt and Salomon offer valuable perspectives, correctives, and cautionary lessons, nonetheless, I am convinced that their emphases and foci are significantly different from those informing this study. That is, Platt and Salomon's data derive either, in the former case, from a peripheral (from Cusco's point of view), incompletely incorporated, non-Inka group in colonial central Bolivia or, in the latter, from local central Peruvian highland community records that appear to date from late colonial to early modern times. The samples of khipu we examine and analyze in this study represent accounts from a (presumed) archaic state administration that was seeking—and in some cases was no doubt more successful than others—to expand its control and influence throughout the central Andean region.

In the process of the state's growth and expansion, the Inka state functionaries, like those in all ancient or modern states, were faced with the challenge of devising some means of information storage and communication. There may well have been some stylistic and procedural differences in local and regional manipulations of the state's principal record-keeping device, the khipu. Nonetheless, *if* the Inka polity did become a state during its brief history (see D'Altroy 2002), it would have been essential to the conduct of state affairs to establish and maintain a mechanism, grounded in shared construction routines and conventional signing values, for storing and exchanging information of state across space and through time. I argue that the Inka did indeed meet this challenge and that the device they relied on for these purposes was the khipu. Our own challenge today is to seek by every means possible to try to understand and appreciate the full range and potential of record keeping that the Inka realized in their use of this device.

Types of Khipu and Forms of Information

It is important at this point to describe the different basic types of khipu that were made and used by the Inka administrators. This relates to an overarching classificatory division among the khipu, and it will therefore be helpful for the reader to be aware from the beginning of this feature of the corpus of material studied. We are told by several of the Spanish chroniclers that the Inka had record keepers for each type of quantitative data or statistical information pertaining to different affairs of state in the empire (see Murúa 1946; Sempat Assadourian 2002). These included (at the least) officials—often termed "secretaries" by the Spaniards—who kept genealogical/historical khipu (Brokaw 1999; Callapiña et al. 1974: 20–22; Julien 1988; Loza 1998; MacCormack 1995; Molina 1916: 58; Rowe 1985; Urton 1990, 1998), as well as astronomical, calendrical, and ritual khipu (Nordenskiöld 1925a, 1925b; Urton 2001; Zuidema 1989). In one particularly complex context, the latter set of linked categories recorded information pertaining to the so-called *ceque* system of Cusco (Bauer 1997; Cobo 1964; Molina 1916: 128; Zuidema 1964). One member of the class of Inka officials specializing in astrological khipu is shown in a drawing by Guaman Poma (Figure 2.3).

When we survey the khipu in various museum collections, we find that the majority appear to have been of the first type mentioned above

2.3. An Inka astrologer with his khipu (Guaman Poma 1980 [1615]: 829 [883]).

—that is, ones that recorded numerical information for statistical record keeping in the Quechua/Inka administrative system of decimal numeration (see Julien 1988). From my own observations of some 450 samples, I have found that approximately two-thirds of the khipu have their knots tied and organized on the strings in a manner so as to sign numerical values. But what of the remaining one-third of the samples? The latter have their knots tied in ways that violate, or are contrary to, the principles of decimal registration procedures (I describe and explain these two forms of registry more thoroughly in Chapter 4). The latter group of khipu represents what I have referred to elsewhere as "anomalous," or "narrative-accounting," khipu (Urton 2002). These are khipu that appear to have been constructed to retain information—perhaps in the form of relatively specific mnemonic notations (e.g., logogram-like units)—for the production of narrative accounts of one kind or another.

The important point to stress in regard to the discussion above is that perhaps the first concern that a khipukamayuq would have attended to in beginning to construct a khipu would have been to answer the question: What type(s) of information will be recorded on this khipu, statistical or narrative? These, I am quick to stress, were *not* mutually exclusive categories, at least not at the level of the totality of information recorded on any given khipu. There are many khipu on which one finds, for instance, a stretch of pendant strings whose knots are organized in a decimal manner associated with a stretch of nondecimal ("anomalous") knot registries. This is consistent with what we see in documents from other ancient writing systems. For instance, in Sumerian cuneiform, Egyptian and Mayan hieroglyphs, and Mycenaean Linear B, we find texts combining statistical data (e.g., the amount of goods sold or bartered; the number of soldiers killed in a battle; or the date of an eclipse) with epic/historical, divinatory, incantatory, or other such poetic and narrative genres. A written document containing these two types of information would combine numerical signs (in whatever base system was in use by the language and culture group in question) with signs or graphemes indicating nouns, verbs, and other grammatical actors. This would be comparable to combining pendants containing decimal and anomalous strings on a single khipu.

In the next section, I address the practical question: What does it mean to "study a khipu?"

The Museum Study of Khipu

The foundation for the study of khipu today is the observations and descriptions of khipu that were made by students of these objects over the years in museums and private collections. The most important body of information to draw on in this regard is the two-volume (microfiche) set of partial tabular descriptions of about 215 khipu samples, entitled *Code of the Quipu: Databooks I and II* (1978), by Marcia and Robert Ascher.[3] The *Databooks* are composed of sample-by-sample tables drawn from the Aschers' careful studies of khipu in museums in Europe and North and South America. The tables are based on a standardized recording format and set of coding symbols for registering systematic observations of certain features of khipu. This information includes:

(1) the assignment of a khipu study number (e.g., for the Aschers, these numbers bear the prefix "AS" [= Ascher]; my own are labeled "UR");

(2) the name and location of the museum in which the sample is located and the catalog number of the sample;

(3) the color of the main (or primary) cord;

(4) a table showing the measurement along the primary cord to each pendant or top string; a sequential numbering of the pendants; measurement of the total length of the primary cord;

(5) observations on each "cord" (i.e., pendant, subsidiary, or top string), including: (a) cord number; (b) the number of knots in each location (esp. decimal numeration level) on the cord; (c) the type of knot(s) on the cord (E = figure-eight knots, L = long knots, S = single knots); (d) total length of the cord; (e) cord color based on a standardized color code; (f) the reading of all knots on the cord for their total decimal value; and (g) the number and location(s) of any subsidiaries attached to the cord; and finally,

(6) any observations on the khipu the researcher wishes to make, such as its association with other khipu, any relevant provenience data, observations on numerical or color patterns, etc.

I earlier characterized the Aschers' *Databook* tables as "partial." What I mean by this is that (as mentioned above) there are several construction features that are not recorded in the *Databook* tables. These include the following observations and types of information:

(7) the material of which the sample is made (usually cotton or wool);

(8) the particular combination of spinning, plying, and wrapping used in the construction of the primary cord;

(9) the directionality of spin and ply of each cord on the khipu;

(10) the direction—front or back (see Chapter 3)—of attachment of each cord to the primary cord; and

(11) the directionality, or manner of actually tying, each knot on the sample to produce either Z- or S-knots (see below).

As should be evident from the above descriptions, each of the construction features identified in items 7–11 is the result of binary decision making and string manipulation. These construction operations are at the heart of the binary khipu code, and it is these features that have never before been systematically collected and reported by researchers.

An example of the tabular recording of all the data deriving from the information and observations described in the two lists above is illustrated in the appendix. This shows the data that were recorded from study of one khipu in the collection in Chachapoyas, from the site of Laguna de los Cóndores, northern Peru (see Urton 2001).

In addition to having spent two summers studying and producing tabular descriptions of the 22 khipu samples that could be studied in Chachapoyas (10 samples were too fragile to study), I have also studied the 300± samples in the Museum für Völkerkunde in Berlin (see Urton 1994) and the 100± samples in the American Museum of Natural History in New York. I note that the Aschers had previously worked in both of these large collections and had therefore already recorded information pertaining to items 1–6 listed above for many samples in these collections. This meant that most of my time in these collections could be devoted to "rereading" the features recorded earlier and recording the additional information for each sample (items 7–11). I have also studied the dozen samples in the Peabody Museum of Archaeology and Ethnology at Harvard University and a couple of samples each in the Textile Museum in Washington and in the Museo Chileno de Arte Precolombino in Santiago de Chile. I estimate that, in all, I have myself studied closely some 450 different khipu. There remain some 200 samples in museums or private collections around the world that have not been studied.

To be somewhat more concrete, if a khipu sample had previously been studied by the Aschers, then my (re)study involved noting the additional pieces of information identified in the second list given above (i.e., items 7–11). If, however, a sample had not been previously studied, it was necessary to record all eleven categories of information noted above and shown in the sample table in the appendix. The amount of time taken to study a khipu for which one must record all eleven items of information for each string and knot obviously varies, depending on the size and complexity of the sample. The study and recording of data from observations of a khipu having only a handful of strings and few knots can be completed within an hour or so. However, at the other end of the spectrum, I recently completed study of a very large (i.e., eighty-eight cords and hundreds of subsidiary strings), colorful, and highly complex woolen khipu in the Museo Chileno de Arte Precolombino in Santiago (see Urton n.d.b). This task consumed fifty hours of work, beginning on Monday morning and ending late Friday afternoon!

It is important to recognize that large bodies of data pertaining to string and knot structures drawn from close observations of binary khipu construction features, like those presented in Chapters 3 and 4, have not been reported in past khipu studies (Conklin [2002] has described all of these forms in detail, but does not himself claim to have documented them with extensive observations). I believe strongly that the best way to approach the study of the khipu is through the description and careful study of variations and patterns in the construction of these remarkable devices. Such an approach is comparable to the way students of other ancient *grapheme*-based script systems take note of minute differences in signing the graphemes by users of those systems (e.g., recognizing slight variations in the marks composing the logosyllabic graphemes of Mayan and Egyptian hieroglyphic texts, or noting the difference between, and the mutually exclusive use of, *b* and *d* in an alphabetic inscription). As Mary Frame has stated the matter:

> The level of distinctions in the Andean code is not so different from the orientation distinctions between letters such as p, b, d, q, which

we master at an early age in order to read and write. Andean children master the basics of Z- and S-twist, number, spin, ply, and reply, in order to participate in the dominant technology of the Andes. (2001: 123)

The Order of Exposition of the System of Binary Coding

We turn in the next chapter to the task of laying out, level by level, the operations undertaken in a process of selecting between two potential ways of constructing the different elements of khipu that resulted in the slow coming together of collections (i.e., of seven layers) of binary-coded features composing each knot on a khipu. I would emphasize before beginning that the order of presenting the various frames of khipu construction will only roughly approximate the order in which I think the operations were actually performed in the construction of any given sample. The order of presentation followed in Chapters 3 and 4 will first take into account what I think the reader may need to know in order to understand the explanation of any given set of techniques and operations; secondly, it will move essentially from the operations that were performed or the decisions that were made in khipu construction for which I have most confidence in my explanations to those about which I am less certain and which I am, therefore, offering primarily as hypotheses.

An example of the latter is color coding. Although the dyeing of threads occurred early in the production of khipu, I have placed my discussion of the binary organization of colors last in my exposition (see Chapter 4). This is because I consider my theory of the binary organization of colors to be the most speculative aspect of the interpretation of the khipu presented in this study. Therefore, in order for the reader to follow—and, I hope, be convinced by—my argument about binary color coding, it will be helpful first to have read evidence pertaining to other, less speculative forms of binary coding in the khipu. In Chapter 5, I produce a diagram that reorders the seven frames, or levels, of manufacturing and decision making in khipu construction in the sequence that I believe would have been followed by a khipukamayuq in actually constructing a khipu. (The reader may wish to look over this model before beginning its exposition; see page 120, Figure 5.2.)

CHAPTER 3

The Physical Components
of Khipu Binary Coding

With the discussions in the previous two chapters as background, we now begin the description of the various components and phases of actually fabricating a khipu by means of performing the seven operations, or stages, of binary decision making and material and string manipulation. The process would have begun, I suggest, with the selection of the construction material.

Materials

In respect to their material composition, khipu are generally made of one or the other of two classes of fibers: cotton or camelid hairs. Cotton was decidedly the material of choice in producing khipu strings, at least as judged by surviving samples, a majority of which are made of cotton. However, there are also many khipu composed wholly of wool threads made from alpaca, llama, or other camelid fibers. Two geographic regions seem to have emphasized the use of wool fibers in khipu construction: the central coast of Peru, at sites around the present-day city of Lima (e.g., Cajamarquilla; see Figure 3.1), and the north coast of Chile, around Arica. I would also note that the ten khipu curated by residents of the central Peruvian highland village of Tupicocha today are composed of wool (Salomon 2002: 301–302). Between these two zones is the region on the south coast of Peru, around Ica and Nazca, from where we have a large concentration of surviving samples of dyed cotton khipu.

In addition to khipu composed entirely of either cotton or woolen threads, there are also samples whose strings are made principally from one or the other of these materials but in which one finds the occasional string spun from the other material. For example, in the predomi-

nately cotton khipu found in Chachapoyas, one often finds admixtures of
woolen strings (see Urton 2001). I
would also note that one occasionally
encounters strings composed of vegetal
fibers as well as of spun and plied human
(or some other animal) hair. It is important to add, however, that the characterization of materials given here is
based on my own observations; though
I am reasonably certain of my identifica-
tions for the majority of samples I have
studied, nonetheless, I am not an expert
in materials, and in many instances it
is very difficult to identify the materials of these archaeological fabrics. To the
best of my knowledge, to date we do
not have a careful study by a materials
expert of the material composition of
khipu in any given collection. This is a
major lacuna in our technical studies of
these objects—one that needs to be addressed as soon as possible.

The use of cotton or wool or (infre-
quently) a combination of these fibers
produced variations in the texture, appearance, and durability of khipu. Both
fiber types may be dyed, although it
is more common in my experience to
find strings made of dyed cotton. I
will take up the question of the dyeing
of strings and the possible meaning of
colors in the khipu in Chapter 4. What is
most important to establish at this point

3.1. Wool khipu from Cajamarquilla (AMNH
B/3453d).

is that the initial set of decisions that a khipukamayuq would have made
in actually beginning to construct a khipu was primarily (though, as we
have seen, not exclusively) binary in nature: Of what material would

each string of the khipu be manufactured—cotton or wool? The answer to this question—as in the case of our analogous binary ASCII code, in which each one of the individual characters making up the eight-bit sequences may be either 1 or 0—could be different from one string to the next on any given sample. This can even theoretically result in the production of khipu having alternating cotton and woolen pendant strings (though I am not aware of such a sample). The point I want to make is that, although khipu are usually made of one or the other of these materials, in theory, each string could be of either substance; thus, a decision about materials was required in constructing each string.

String Construction—The Spinning and Plying of Threads

With a few exceptions (e.g., Arellano 1999; Conklin 2002; Salomon 2002; Urton 1994, 2001, 2002), previous studies of khipu have had little to say regarding the actual construction or manufacture of strings from raw fibers. I am referring here to the spinning and plying of yarns, as well as to the manipulation of strings in knotting. As we will see, each of these khipu construction procedures proceeded in a binary manner. To take up first the topic of spinning and plying, these operations may be performed—using the drop spindle that was (and still is) common throughout much of the Andes—with either a clockwise, rightward motion, which produces Z-spun or -plied threads, *or* with a counterclockwise, leftward motion to produce S-spun or -plied threads.[1] "Z" and "S" refer to the orientation of fibers in the manufactured threads; that is, the threads may run obliquely either from upper right to lower left, like the central line of the letter Z, or they may run from upper left to lower right, like the central line of the letter S (see Minar 2000: 86–88; Seiler-Baldinger 1994: 3–4).

Though one must generally examine a thread closely to determine the direction of spinning, the direction of plying threads together is usually easy to see as well as to feel. However, it should be understood that the first operation of spinning raw fibers into threads and the second one of plying threads into strings will, virtually without exception, be in opposite directions. That is, Z-spun fibers will always be S-plied into threads, and S-spun fibers will become Z-plied threads (see Figure 3.2). The explanation for the opposed directions of spinning and plying is that as the oppositely spun and plied fibers respond to the natural forces to unwind (i.e., in opposite directions), they will reinforce each other, thereby producing greater tensile strength in the finished strings.

When we study the actual patterns of spinning and plying of strings in the khipu, we find that, as in Inka textiles more generally, there is an overwhelming preference for the combination Z-spun/S-plied (see Frame 2001: 116; A. Rowe 1997: 6). Of the 208 khipu in Berlin, New York, and Peru (Chachapoyas) for which I have noted spin and ply directionality, 190 samples (91.3%) contain all Z-spun/S-plied strings. Of the remaining samples, 5 (2.4%) have all S-spun/Z-plied strings, and 13 (6.2%) have some combination of Z-spun/S-plied and S-spun/Z-plied strings (see Urton 1994).

I want to make two general observations on the topic of spinning and plying directions. First, although the individuals who constructed the khipu strings presumably had two equally viable options (speaking in terms of the integrity of string construction) for spin and ply directions, the decisions they actually made on this matter, as displayed in the construction of the thousands of strings composing the 208 khipu whose spin and ply directions I have recorded, were overwhelmingly in line with thread construction in Inka textile production more generally—that is, they were predominantly Z-spun/S-plied. This means that there was a high degree of continuity between khipu and textiles in the manufacturing of cloth products in the empire. Thus, the khipu were not aberrant products of Inka fabric technology. And second, if we seek an

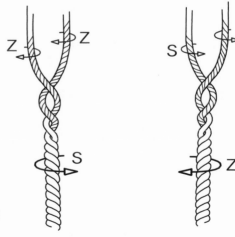

3.2. Two styles of spinning and plying with a drop spindle.

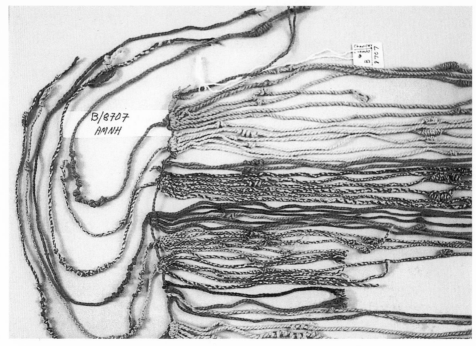

3.3. Khipu from Chancay-Huando (AMNH B/8707).

entry into Inka modes of signing complex narratives, as opposed to the more common and—speaking in terms of their apparent format—standardized decimal-based khipu, we may be well advised to focus attention on those "anomalous" samples whose strings either are constructed wholly "contrary to the norm" (i.e., S-spun/Z-plied) or have mixed spinning and plying directions. I will present just such an analysis of one of the most spectacular examples of an "anomalous" S-spun/Z-plied khipu (AMNH B/8705) in Chapter 4.

An interesting example of a khipu displaying "mixed" string construction—that is, one that combines Z-spun/S-plied with S-spun/Z-plied threads—is sample B/8707, from the American Museum of Natural History (see Figure 3.3). The provenience of this sample is given in museum records as the Chancay-Huando region on the central coast of Peru. Figure 3.4 provides a schematic rendering of this khipu with notations indicating spin/ply directions.

In Figure 3.4, *S* indicates a Z-spun/*S*-plied string, whereas a *Z* inside a circle indicates a string that is made of S-spun/*Z*-plied threads. Although the majority of pendant and top strings on Khipu B/8707 are Z-spun/

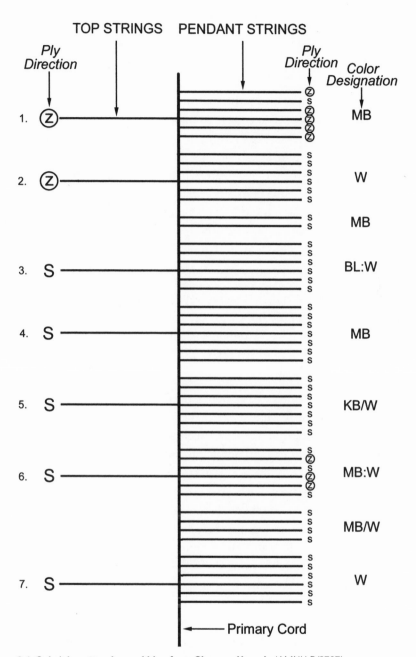

3.4. Spin/ply patterning on khipu from Chancay-Huando (AMNH B/8707).

S-plied, several are S-spun/Z-plied. The latter include Top Strings Nos. 1 and 2; five of the six pendant strings associated with Top String No. 1; and three of the six pendant strings associated with Top String No. 6.

It is clear that variation in spin and ply directionality was being used in the construction of Khipu B/8707 in some manner, which I cannot now explain, to classify the information on this device into at least two different categories. As a suggestion, it could be that the information encoded in the S-spun/Z-plied strings provides narrative commentary on, or exceptions to, the information provided in the Z-spun/S-plied strings. Another possible explanation could be that such variation might signal some aspect of the status (e.g., gender or ethnic identity) of the khipukamayuq or of the information signed in the knot record. For example, Gerardo Reichel-Dolmatoff noted that among the Kogi of northern Colombia,

> . . . the twist [i.e., final ply direction] depends on the sex of the individual who is spinning: the men twist to the left, that is to say, from the knee toward the body, and women to the right, with a movement from the body toward the knee. (1949–1950: 61; cited in Minar 2000: 98)

Most of the examples of S-spun/Z-plied khipu—that is, those produced in the "contrary" direction—that I am familiar with and for which we have data concerning their provenience come from sites along the central coast of Peru (e.g., Chancay, Huando, and Pachacamac); few of these khipu derive from the northern highlands (Chachapoyas) or from either of the important south coastal Peruvian khipu proveniences of Ica and Nazca. Thus, it is also possible that the variation that we do see in khipu string manufacturing may have had some relationship to different regional or ethnic traditions of khipu construction. In this regard, it is interesting to note for comparative purposes that in their review of the distribution of different patterns of spinning and plying directionality among forty-one different groups in the Amazon basin, James B. Petersen and Jack A. Wolford (2000) found that variation in this binary construction feature often distinguished neighboring populations that have traditionally been differentiated on the basis of ethnicity or linguistic affiliation.

I would also mention here the extremely interesting information on variation in spinning and plying directionality described by Frank Salomon from his study of the ten khipu of the present-day village of Tupicocha. Salomon found that the khipu tend to be organized into paired sets that, in turn, are linked to paired sets of *ayllu;* these are the social, political, and ritual groupings by which residents in the village are organized. As Salomon noted with respect to one of these paired sets of *ayllu* and khipu:

> . . . the originally paired set consisting of specimens 1SF-01 and 2SF-01, that is, the pair that belonged to undivided Ayllu Satafasca until the 1920s, contrasts in cord directionality. Quipocamayo [i.e., the Tupicochan term for *khipu*] 2SF-01, which belongs to the junior segment, is overwhelmingly Z-plied, and its counterpart, 1SF-01, of the senior segment, is overwhelmingly S-plied. (2002: 305)

Handedness and Semiotic Intentionality

Before we discuss other physical characteristics of khipu construction resulting from the binary manipulation of strings in space and time, there is one general topic of concern that will, I fear, undermine and bedevil our entire conversation if it is not addressed directly here. This is the matter of handedness. This problem, which may already have occurred to the reader in the above discussion of spin and ply directionality, will also present complications for our discussion of directionality in the attachment of strings to primary cords, as well as in the knotting of khipu pendant strings. In all of these contexts, we will find that the appearance of the physical constructions (e.g., the knot topologies and orientations of thread axes) resulting from many of these operations will mimic differences that we ourselves can reproduce by performing the operations in question with either the right or the left hand. Our suspicion might well be, then, that what I am describing here as patterns of variation and difference in thread manipulations as core processes of a system of signing and communication are, perhaps, nothing more than natural products of differences in handedness among the people making up any given population. I strongly suspect that, by the end of this chapter, the reader will agree with me that the patterns we see in these variations are too suggestive to attribute to accident, or to an absence of intentionality. However, we should consider certain data that help us make a coherent argument for intentionality, rather than leaving the matter to chance.

One of the few studies I am aware of that directly addresses the question of directionality and the manipulation of threads is C. Jill Minar's (2000) investigation of handedness and spin/ply directionality among a group of forty-three spinners (Minar assembled her subject group through a questionnaire submitted to *Spin Off* magazine and the Internet; 2000: 88–89). Beginning with the hypothesis that spinning direction may be linked to handedness, Minar notes that conventional wisdom (and studies by psychologists) suggests that about 80–90 percent of people are right-handers and 10–20 percent are left-handers (2000: 92). Minar found, in fact, that this was almost exactly confirmed in her study sample of forty-three spinners, in which 86 percent were right-handers and 14 percent were left-handers. As for usual directionality in spinning and plying, Minar found among her group of spinners that 88 percent usually spun Z and plied S, whereas 12 percent spun S and plied Z. On the surface, these numbers would seem to confirm a link between handedness and directionality of spinning (i.e., the 86% of right-handers would produce the 88% of Z-spun/S-plied threads). However, when she studied her sample group as individuals (rather than looking at the aggregate percentages), Minar found that normal spin/ply directionality did *not* correlate with handedness. That is, all the left-handers spun and plied like the majority of right-handers (i.e., Z/S), and five (12%) of the right-handers spun and plied in the opposite direction (S/Z)!

When she looked at several other factors, Minar concluded that the principal factor determining the directionality of spin and ply was the learning process; that is, spinners usually spin and ply in the same manner as their teachers. This results in what Minar (citing Lave and Wenger 1991) refers to as "communities of practice." A second important consideration was the cultural ideas and symbolic values associated by a particular population with doing things a certain way and, conversely, with reversing the usual directions; the latter was considered, among spinners, to be either bad luck or particularly powerful, significant, or sacred in some manner (Minar 2000: 92–98).

I argue that these two explanatory points are critical and generalizable and that they should form the basis for our thinking about handedness, intentionality, and meaning in patterns of construction in the khipu. That is, I contend that the variation we see in khipu construction is the result of intentional, meaning-laden choices about doing things one way or the other among a group of people—the khipukama-yuq—that formed a "community of practice." Thus, I am returning to my earlier point that the people who made these knotted-string devices knew what they were doing, and they did what they did in fabricating these complicated objects for meaningful reasons, not because they happened to be right-handed or left-handed. Furthermore, I want to say in this regard that, in my own experience of having lived for some five years in communities in various regions of the Andes, overt left-handedness (i.e., as opposed to a loose ambidexterity or overt right-handedness) is quite rare. In fact, I do not recall knowing a single left-handed person, especially not in any of the rural farming communities I have studied and lived in. I have also often observed that children in these communities are instructed in writing with the right hand (i.e., pointedly being discouraged from using the left hand). And finally, the right hand is accorded symbolic priority in every ritual and symbolic setting that I am aware of today, and this is reflected as well in the colonial historical literature characterizing Inka ritualism and symbolism (e.g., Classen 1993: 12–13, 22–23). Thus, when people use the right or the left hand, or when they apply values of "rightness" and "leftness" to phenomena in their world, they do and say what they intend. I propose that we assume the same to have been true of the khipukamayuq when they constructed the knotted-string records.

Mode of Attachment of Strings to Primary Cords

During a study begun in the summer of 1998 of a collection of thirty-two khipu recently discovered in Chachapoyas, northern Peru (see Urton 2001),[2] I became aware of a significant degree of variation in the way khipu pendant strings are attached to primary cords. As is true of other construction features, this variation constitutes a binary manipulation, or "coding," of the khipu structure. I have recorded information on variations in string attachments on twenty-one of the twenty-two khipu samples from this collection whose state of preservation permits close examination. As I did not become aware of the variation in this component of khipu construction until I began work on the Chachapoya khipu, I did not record this information for any of the samples

3.5. Pendant attachments to primary cord (recto face; Museum für Völkerkunde, Berlin, VA 47076).

studied earlier in the collections in Berlin or New York (e.g., Urton 1994). Therefore, much more work in the form of careful observations on these latter two particularly large museum collections remains to be done before this particular feature of khipu construction can be adequately documented.

In general terms, strings are attached to primary cords by what is known as a "half-hitch" knot (Figure 3.5). These knots are produced by first opening up one end of the plied pendant string; the opposite (unopened) end of the string is passed around the primary cord and then down through the opened end of the string; finally, the string is pulled taut to secure its place on the primary cord (see Conklin 2002: Figure 3.26). There are two different ways of performing this operation in assembling khipu, which I have designated as *recto* (= r) and *verso* (= v).[3] These two modes of string-attachment technique and the visual differences produced by them in the appearance of strings attached to primary cords on khipu are illustrated in Figure 3.6a and b.

It will immediately be apparent to the reader that the recto and verso designations for any given string attachment will be reversed depending on the side of the khipu from which one views that attachment. Al-

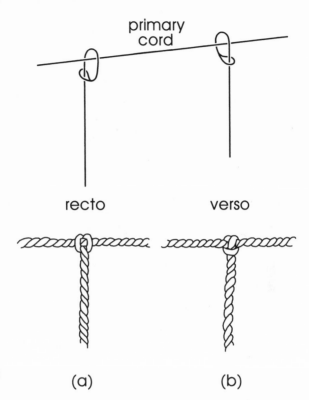

primary
cord

recto   verso

3.6. Recto (= a) and verso (= b) pendant attachments.   (a)   (b)

though this is certainly true, nonetheless, what is important to note is that *oppositely* attached strings will always be *different* from each other in their attachment, regardless of how the two types of attachments are designated in our nomenclature.

The critical point to recognize with respect to any possible syntactic or semantic significance that might have been assigned to differences in string attachments is that at what would have been an early stage of manufacturing a khipu—the attaching of strings to the primary cord—binary decisions were being made with respect to the nature, or classification, of the information being recorded or represented on the khipu. The "nature" of that material could be identified as either: (a) all of one type (i.e., undifferentiated at this initial level), in which case the strings would all be attached in either verso or recto fashion; or (b) two different types, one designated by the verso attachment, the other by the recto attachment. The question now is: What patterns do we actually see in the only sampling of khipu (to my knowledge) for which this information has been systematically recorded—that is, in the twenty-one Chachapoya samples? This information is shown in Table 3.1.

As is clear from the information presented in Table 3.1, the majority of khipu studied in the collection from Chachapoyas have a "mixed recto/verso" pattern of pendant attachment. The designation of these khipu as displaying "mixed" patterns decidedly downplays what are, in fact, a number of exceptionally interesting and quite complex forms of organizing and classifying information by string-attachment patterns on certain of these samples. Although there is not space here to note in detail the patterns on all of the fourteen khipu in Table 3.1 whose attachment patterns are designated as mixed, it is nonetheless important and valuable to look at a couple of examples. This will be helpful in order to establish the central point that I want to communicate in the discussion in this section: pendant attachments in the khipu are quite varied, and thus must have been an important mode of binary coding in the khipu.

Two pendant-attachment patterns—for Khipu UR2 and UR5[4]—are illustrated in Table 3.2.

I should inform the reader that, on the basis of my complete study of the physical features of the two khipu represented in Table 3.2, there are no (at least obvious) coincidences between either the spatial grouping of pendants along the primary cords or the color patterning of pendants on Khipu UR2 and UR5 and the pendant-attachment patterns that are documented in Table 3.2. Looking at the attachment patterns themselves, we see a range of one to eleven strings having one or the other (in alternation) of the verso/recto pendant-attachment forms.

The principal conclusion that we can draw from the data provided in Tables 3.1 and 3.2 is that string attachment—the principal act of khipu assembly—indeed appears to have conveyed some type(s) of "information" (i.e., differences resulting from processes of decision making) in the khipu recording system. Unfortunately, we cannot say at present precisely what kind of information was signed in this way. It is hoped that investigators will begin to record these variations and that we will, thereby, have an increasing body of information on this feature of khipu construction in order to begin to study the relationships between string attachment and other forms of patterning (such as color, knot directionality, etc.) characterizing groups of strings or whole khipu. In this way,

TABLE 3.1.
Pendant Attachments on Khipu from Laguna de los Cóndores
(Chachapoyas)

Khipu Designation		No. of Pendants in Sample	Recto	Verso	Mixed r/v
UR1		386			*
UR2		69			*
UR4		441			*
UR5		47			*
UR6		754			*
UR7		45			*
UR8		6		*	
UR9		143			*
UR10		157			*
UR11		176		79–118	1–78; 119–176
UR12		45			*
UR13		22	1–7; 22	8–21	
UR14		20			*
UR15		62	1–6; 52–62	7–51	
UR16		220	*		
UR17		84			*
UR18		27			*
UR19		13			*
UR20		22			*
UR21		133	11–19	1–10; 27–104	20–26
UR22*	-a	94	29–31	1–28; 32–94	
	-b	70	10–70	1–9	
	-c	96	*		
	-f	6		*	

* UR22 is a khipu with strings pendant from a 25.5 cm long bar. The pendant strings are attached along three of the long sides of the bar (sides a, b, and c) and one end (f).

TABLE 3.2.
Pendant-Attachment Patterns on Two Khipu from Laguna de los Cóndores
(Chachapoyas)

Khipu Identification	String Attachments	
	Verso	Recto
UR2	1—3	4
	5—7	8—10
	11—12	13—16
	17–27	28–32
	33–36	37
	38–47	48
	49–50	51–52
	53–59	60–63
	64–67	68
	[69–?]*	
UR5	1–3	4
	5	6–10
	11–12	13–18
	19–20	21–22
	23–28	29–34
	35	36–41
	42–44	45–46
	47	

* Pendant attachment could not be read.

we may eventually identify larger, more inclusive structural patterns in the ways these devices were actually assembled.

Knot Directionality

When we turn to the topic of directional variation in knotting, we encounter an even more varied and complicated picture than we saw with either string construction or pendant attachment, but one that nevertheless constitutes still another expression of binary coding. It will be helpful to first clarify how directional variability comes about in knot construction.

It has long been recognized that there are three principal types of knots tied into khipu pendant strings; these have been designated as figure-eight knots, long knots, and single knots (Locke 1923). For those khipu that can be shown to have recorded quantitative data in the place notation system of decimal numeration employed by Inka administrators, the three knot types had the following functions:

figure-eight knots	indicated single units (i.e., 1s)
long knots	indicated the units 2–9
single knots	indicated 10s, 100s, 1,000s, or 10,000s (depending on placement)

There are actually two ways of constructing each one of the three principal knot types identified above; these differing constructions result in what I have referred to elsewhere as "Z-knots" and "S-knots" (Urton 1994).[5] In the simplest terms, these two knot types are characterized by the dominant diagonal axis of the knot that crosses the plane of the pendant string going *either* from upper right to lower left (/ = Z-knot) *or* from upper left to lower right (\ = S-knot). Figure 3.7 shows a pair of S- and Z-tied long knots; Figure 3.8 shows a series of four S-tied single knots.

These two knot variations are produced by certain regular combinations of front/back and right/left manipulations of strings in the construction of knots. To clarify this point, Figure 3.9 illustrates the initial string movements for making Z-knots, and Figure 3.10 shows those motions for making S-knots. The procedures in both cases involve moving the free, unattached end of a string (i.e., the end of the string not attached to the primary cord) either from right to left or left to right, in back of (or behind) the upper part of the string or in front of it. Specifically, as we see in Figure 3.9, *Z-knots* result from moving the lower, free end of a string either from right to left behind the main body of the string or from left to right in front of the string. On the other hand, *S-knots* result from moving the free end of the string either from left to right behind the upper string or from right to left in front of the upper string (see Figure 3.10). These alternative methods of producing Z- and S-knots describe the initial but defining movements in knot construction.

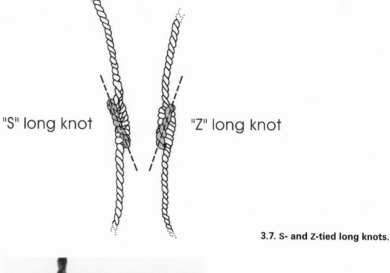

"S" long knot   "Z" long knot

3.7. S- and Z-tied long knots.

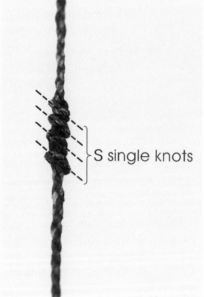

S single knots

3.8. Set of four S-tied single knots
(Museum für Völkerkunde, Berlin, VA
16140).

As will be obvious from a moment's reflection, each of the paired procedures shown in Figures 3.9 and 3.10 represent the *same* operations but as viewed from opposite sides of the string. For instance, the two ways to produce S-knots represent two points of view, turned 180° from each other, on a *single* operation. Despite the fact that these two

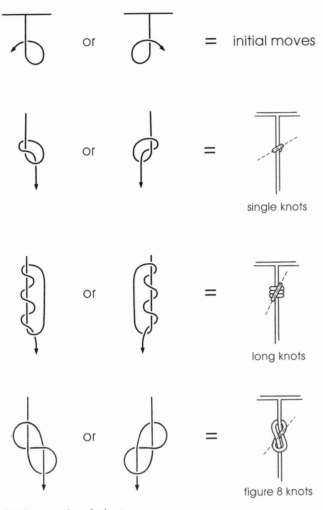

= initial moves

= single knots

= long knots

= figure 8 knots

3.9. Construction of Z-knots.

sets of paired operations are reversible and reciprocal, it is nonetheless important to bear in mind that the khipu maker who undertook to make either a Z- or an S-knot had two different manipulative procedures available for producing the same kind of knot.

A few general comments are in order at this point concerning the possibility that the meticulous descriptions of variations in knot types provided above may give the reader the impression that this is perhaps a lot of fine hair-splitting over what may represent, after all, rather insig-

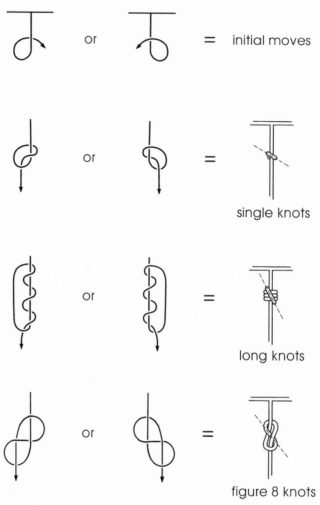

or = initial moves

or = single knots

or = long knots

or = figure 8 knots

3.10. Construction of S-knots.

nificant or unimportant differences in the construction and appearance of khipu knots. I would argue in two ways that this would be a significant misinterpretation of the importance of these construction features and their variations for the khipu coding system.

Speaking first at the level of practice—that is, in terms of a khipukamayuq's manipulation of strings in producing these knots—if one takes a piece of string and reproduces the various operations described in Figures 3.9 and 3.10, it will immediately become apparent that a good deal of thought and concentration, as well as a considerable number of unusual, if not uncomfortable, bodily motions, are required to produce Z- and S-varieties of each of the three knot types. Even granting the gradual accommodation of the body and the senses to these unusual and complex procedures in manipulating strings—a process of habituation that must have been a hallmark of a khipukamayuq's development and maturation—the khipukamayuq would doubtlessly have remained profoundly aware and deeply conscious of his/her various bodily movement and tactile sensations in reproducing the different types and variants of knots described above. Therefore, I argue not only that variations in knot directionality were the results of deliberate, conscious, and meaningful actions, but also that the body of knowledge and habitus that produced them would have been central or core elements in the arts of recording and reading performed by khipukamayuq by means of the khipu.

Second, and speaking now at the level of our present-day experience of the products of the procedural variations described above—that is, from our actual viewing or study of the khipu knots—the Z- and S-variants of the three different types of knots are, in fact, quite easily recognizable. In my own experience, I found in my month-long study of the collection in Berlin, for instance, that after staring intently at strings and knots on a couple of hundred khipu for some seven hours a day, five days a week, for a month, in glancing at a khipu a few meters away, I could easily note the presence of most of the knot type variants (i.e., Z- or S-) described above.

In short, though the descriptions of variants of knot types presented above may strike the reader as ponderous—the unfortunate, but perhaps inevitable, consequence of translating visual and tactile information and experiences into words—I would argue that these string manipulations and their products were of vital interest to the people who made and consulted the khipu. In fact, the knot variants represented the final "spin" that was given to information recorded by khipukamayuq on this extraordinary device. Therefore, it is not only essential that we take into account variations in knot directionality in our attempts to interpret the khipu, but also that we do so with the awareness that knot variation probably represented one of the last actions performed by khipukamayuq in their production of a khipu.

There is tremendous variability in the patterning and distribution of S- and Z-knots in khipu samples in the various museum collections I have studied to date. Space does not permit a complete description and analysis of all of the material on variability in patterning of knot directionality. However, as this construction feature was so critical to the binary coding/signing system used in the khipu, it is vital that we view a summary of the patterns of knot variation distribution identified in the collections studied thus far, as well as discuss a few of the ways variation in knot directionality organizes information in the khipu. The summary data are presented in Table 3.3.

Table 3.3 was assembled on the basis of information collected in the course of study of khipu in museum collections in Peru, Germany, and the United States.[6] To clarify the information presented in Table 3.3, the three columns on the left-hand side of the table, under the heading "Knot Combinations," represent different patterns in the distribution of S- and Z-tied single, long, and figure-eight knots. This is the order these knots assume as they are arrayed from the top (i.e., where the pendant string is attached to the primary cord) to the bottom of strings on statistical, or numerical-accounting, khipu (see below). For example, reading across the top line of Table 3.3, a khipu having this particular combination of knots would have all its single, long, and figure-eight knots tied as Z-knots (or there would be no figure-eight knots in the sample). The numbers under the central columns of the table, labeled with capital letters (A, B, C, . . .), represent the different proveniences, or provenience zones, from which khipu samples derived; numbers in these columns give the total number of samples in the collections studied that bear the knot-combination patterns in question. As will be seen from the key to the provenience zones at the foot of the table, proveniences are organized from the northern highlands (A = Chachapoyas) to the south coast (G) of Peru. The right-hand column gives the total number of samples in the collections displaying each of the knot-combination patterns identified.

As we see in Table 3.3, all knots on 50 (29.6%) of the 169 khipu samples for which I have recorded this information were tied as Z-knots. In 24 of the 169 samples (i.e., 14.2%), all knots were tied as S-knots. What is interesting to note is that the majority of khipu—95 of 169 samples (56.2%)—display some combination of S- and Z-knots in their construction. Elsewhere, I have described and illustrated certain pat-

TABLE 3.3.
Patterns of Variability in Knot Directionality Organized by Provenience Zones

Knot Combinations			Provenience Zone*								Total
Single	Long	Figure-8	A	B	C	D	E	F	G	H	
Z	Z	Z/blank**	2	11	11	1	17	3	5	—	50
Z	Z	Z/S	3	1	1	—	1	—	—	—	6
Z	blank	blank	—	—	4	2	1	—	—	—	7
Z	S/Z	S/Z	1	—	—	—	—	—	—	—	1
Z	S/Z	Z/blank	1	—	3	—	—	—	—	—	4
Z	Z	S	2	1	1	4	8	—	—	—	16
Z	S	Z	—	—	6	—	2	—	—	—	8
Z	S	S	—	—	—	—	—	—	—	1	1
Z	S	blank	—	—	8	—	—	—	—	—	8
blank	S	S	—	—	1	—	—	—	—	—	1
blank	S/Z	S/Z/blank	2	—	—	—	—	—	—	—	2
blank	S	blank	—	1	—	—	—	—	—	—	1
blank	Z	S/Z	—	—	—	1	—	—	—	—	1
S	S	S/blank	4	2	2	5	5	6	—	—	24
S	S	S/Z	1	1	—	1	—	—	1	—	4
S	S	Z	—	1	1	—	6	—	—	—	8
blank	S	Z	—	—	1	—	1	—	—	—	2
S	Z	blank	—	—	—	—	1	—	—	—	1
S	S/Z	S	—	1	—	—	—	—	—	—	1
S	S/Z	Z	—	—	—	—	—	—	1	—	1
S/Z	S/Z	S/Z/blank	3	1	6	—	2	4	—	1	17
S/Z	S	S	1	—	—	—	—	—	1	—	2
S/Z	S	Z	—	—	—	1	—	—	—	—	1
S/Z	Z	S/Z/blank	2	—	—	—	—	—	—	—	2
										Total	169

* *Provenience Zones:* A Chachapoyas (Laguna de los Cóndores)
                                 B Lima north to Huacho
                                   C Pachacamac
                                   D Cajamarquilla
                                   E Ica/Pisco
                                   F Nazca
                                   G South Coast
                                   H Unknown
** "Blank" indicates that there are no knots of this type in the sample(s).

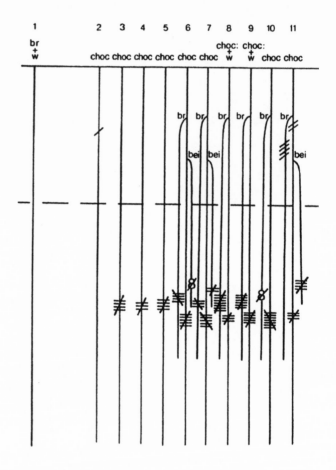

terns found in the distribution of S- and Z-knots in a few khipu bearing both knot types (see Urton 1994). These include samples having, for example, a seemingly random mix of the two knot types (Figure 3.11), as well as samples having one-half (or virtually that proportion) of their knots tied as S-knots and the other half tied as Z-knots (Figure 3.12). These are not uncommon forms of knot combinations in the samples studied.

It should be noted that there do not appear to be any compelling regional patterns that emerge in the frequency of any one of the knot-combination patterns among the various provenience zones shown in Table 3.3. Thus, it does not appear, at least not from the data assembled to date, that we could develop regional, ethnic, or linguistic taxonomies

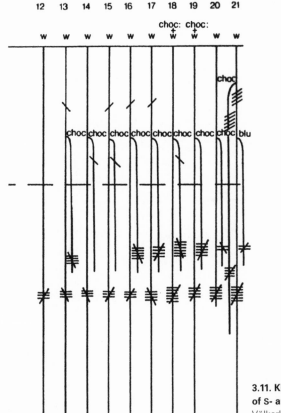

3.11. Khipu with random assortment of S- and Z-knots (Museum für Völkerkunde, Berlin, no number).

of khipu types, or styles, based solely on the geographical distribution of Z- or S-knots or on certain type-variety configurations of knots.

I will present here one additional example in order to help the reader appreciate how the distribution and patterning of S- and Z-knots can organize and modify the information in a khipu in quite complex and interesting ways (see Figure 3.13). The sample shown in Figure 3.13 was recovered from the coastal Peruvian site of Pachacamac, which is located just to the south of the present-day city of Lima.[7] Figure 3.14 is a schematic diagram of the khipu shown in Figure 3.13.

The khipu shown in Figure 3.13 and illustrated in Figure 3.14 is composed of a primary cord and twenty-one pendant strings, the latter of which are all of Z-spun/S-plied undyed cotton. This khipu contains

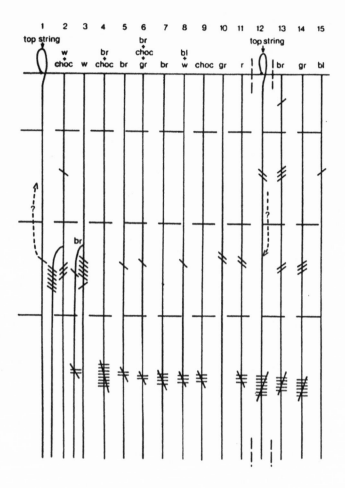

some very large numerical values, with knots tied in layers denoting ones, tens, one hundreds, one thousands, and ten thousands. When we look at the actual construction (i.e., the tying) of knots in this sample, we find that the distribution of the two knot types (S- and Z-) produces a division of this khipu into *quarters*. The vertical axis of the four-part division of this khipu falls within a narrow space between the seventh and eighth pendant strings, and the horizontal axis runs along the line dividing the ones position (i.e., composed of figure-eight and long knots) from the single knots denoting successively higher powers of ten. As determined by these two axes of division, we note that all single knots in the upper left-hand quadrant, as well as the long knots and figure-eight

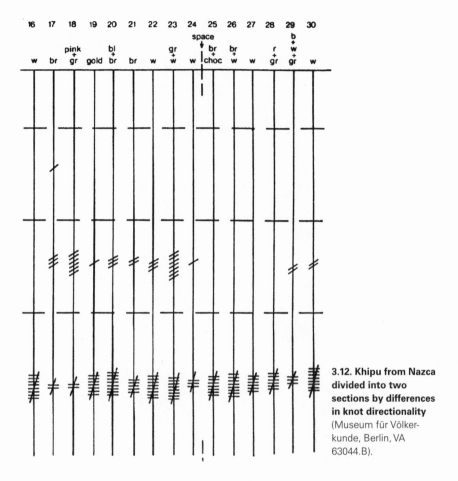

3.12. Khipu from Nazca divided into two sections by differences in knot directionality (Museum für Völkerkunde, Berlin, VA 63044.B).

knots in the lower right-hand quadrant, are tied as *S-knots;* all knots in the upper right-hand quadrant and those in the lower left-hand quadrant are tied as *Z-knots.*

It is a curious fact and probably no more than a coincidence that the orientations of the oblique axes of placement of the two knot types (i.e., Zs in the upper right and lower left; Ss in the upper left and lower right) coincide with the respective oblique axes of the knots themselves (see the schematic diagram at the bottom of Figure 3.14). One might, for instance, construct an argument to the effect that this coincidence of axes might have served in some manner to establish the "handedness," or perhaps the direction of reading, of this khipu.

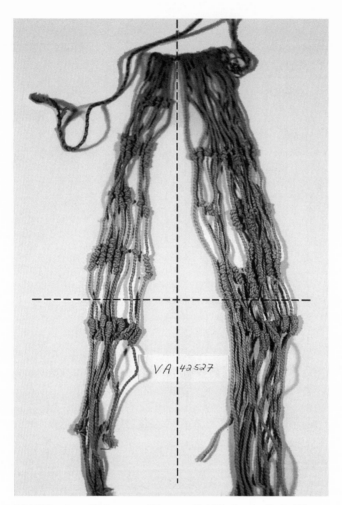

3.13. Khipu from Pachacamac (Museum für Völkerkunde, Berlin, VA 42527).

What could have been the meaning of the four-part organization of the information tied into the khipu illustrated in Figure 3.14? Could the observed patterning in knot directionality be as direct a reflection of the Inka emphasis—their "insistence"—on duality and quadripartite socio-political organization as it appears on the surface? Or, somewhat more specifically in relation to Inka communicative and accounting practices, would we be justified in arguing that the information in the paired quadrants (as determined by the distribution of S- and Z-knots) should be

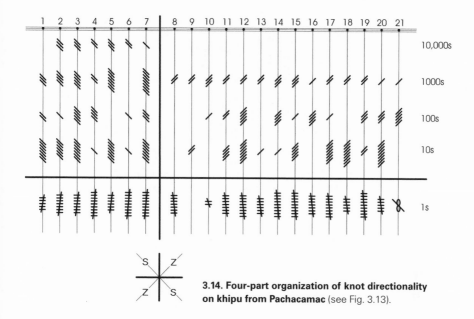

3.14. Four-part organization of knot directionality on khipu from Pachacamac (see Fig. 3.13).

read together—that is, reading the S-knots in the upper-left quadrant together with those in the lower-right quadrant—rather than simply reading down the full length of each string, from top to bottom?

I would also raise the highly speculative question of whether or not the pattern of knotting in Figure 3.14 could represent a convention for registering decimal values. That is, on all strings, the numbers in what we normally refer to as the ones place are all tied differently from those in the tens and higher places. Could the ones values have represented decimals, the tens therefore having been ones, and so on up the length of the strings? For example, according to this recording principle, we might read Pendant No. 1, which has the following knot quantities (going from the top to the bottom of the string): 3/2/7/5, as 327.5; Pendant No. 2 would represent 3,416.7, and so on. I would conclude this speculation by noting that we have very little experience in interpreting such formats, or structural patterns, based as they are on a binary construction feature of the khipu (i.e., knot directionality) that has heretofore gone largely unreported.

The important lessons to be learned from the example presented above (and those published elsewhere; Urton 1994) about the organization of information according to knot directionality are, first, that variability in the construction of knots resulting in Z- and S-knots was an important binary-coding element of the khipu information system. Second, we need to catalogue and study closely such patterns as those seen in Figures 3.11, 3.12, and 3.14 in order to enlarge and further refine our knowledge and understanding of patterning in the construction and distribution of khipu knots. Only in this way can we begin to articulate better hypotheses and paradigms for directing future studies of the encoding signs and information systems of these remarkable recording devices. And third, the message seems clear that, at the very least, we need to begin to revise our approach to the study of quantitative values recorded on khipu. That is, a long knot of six turns is no longer simply that quantitative value (i.e., 6); rather, such a knot ought henceforth to be considered as either an *S* six or a *Z* six.

In the course of this chapter, we have examined four of the string-processing and -manipulation procedures that went into the early phases of khipu construction. These were the procedures of materials selection, the spinning and plying of fibers, the attachment of strings to primary cords, and the tying of knots into pendant strings. In the next chapter, we will turn to two aspects of khipu construction that will challenge our contention that all recording features of the khipu were premised on the binary organization of information and manipulation of strings in the khipu information system; these relate to the more abstract qualities known as numbers and colors.

CHAPTER 4

The Linguistic Components
of Khipu Binary Coding

In this chapter, we turn first to the question of the organization of numbers in Quechua, which was the lingua franca and language of administration in the Inka Empire (see Mannheim 1991). This is obviously a large, complex subject and therefore one to which we cannot do full justice within the confines of the present study (see Urton 1997). Nonetheless, it is important to analyze the ways in which numbers—the multitermed continuum par excellence for modifying, classifying, and organizing relations between objects in the world (being matched in this respect perhaps only by colors)—can be understood to have been organized and deployed, surprisingly, as elements of a system of *binary* coding in the Inka khipu.

When we closely analyze ideas about numbers as reflected in the syntax and semantics of everyday discourse, as well as in formal and technical language settings (e.g., in conversing about warping and weaving textiles) evoking number sets, series, proportionality, and so on in Quechua, we find that the "integers" (Quechua *yupana, yupaykuna* = 1, 2, 3, . . .) are organized at their most basic level in terms of the alternation between what are considered to be two related *social* states of being: *ch'ulla* (odd; alone) and *ch'ullantin* (even; pair; the odd one together with its natural partner). The most elementary numerical expression of the *ch'ulla/ch'ullantin* relationship is that between *uj* (one) and *iskay* (two). Note, however, that this is not an *additive* relationship, as is the case with the number sentence: 1 + 1 = 2. Rather, the *ch'ulla/ch'ullantin* relationship, which in Quechua is a—if not *the*—paradigm of numerical organization, is premised on the sequence of the integers in which *sets* are formed by linking each odd/*ch'ulla* number (1, 3, 5, . . .) together with its even/*ch'ullantin* complement (respectively: 2,

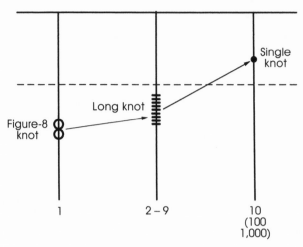

4.1. Khipu knot signs and their numerical values.

4, 6) to form complete number sets. Therefore, the number sentence for the primal version of the *ch'ulla/ch'ullantin* relationship is: "one united with two produces the paired set (1–2)." Thus, throughout the number series, numbers are conceived of by Quechua speakers as produced and organized in binary (odd/even) pairs. This is analogous to ASCII code, in which, for instance, each unit in a coded sequence is either 1 or 0.

The structures and organizing principles of Quechua numeration outlined above are also evident in the system of signing numbers (and perhaps other values or meanings) in the khipu. I should state to begin with that I do not pretend to be exhaustive in my discussion of the registration and organization of numbers in the khipu. My main purpose is to explore the logic of signing numbers in the numerical-statistical khipu in general. The specific question that I address below is whether or not, in addition to its importance in Quechua numerical ontology (as discussed above and in Urton 1997), *binary* coding was also an organizing principle in techniques for registering *decimal* numerical values in the khipu.

The first point to make with regard to the registration of numbers in the khipu concerns the economy of types of signs used (see Figure 4.1). As mentioned earlier, there are three major sign types: *figure-eight knots,* indicating ones (i.e., single units); *long knots,* which signify the units from 2 to 9; and *single knots,* which, depending on their position on a string, may signify any one of the full decimal units (i.e., 10s, 100s, 1,000s, or 10,000s).

As viewed from the point of attachment of the khipu pendant string with the primary cord, one encounters, in moving down the body of the string, single knots tied on successively lower levels, indicating decreasing powers of ten; then one encounters *either* (a) a long knot, signifying units from 2 to 9, followed by a space (where the figure-eight knot would otherwise stand), *or* (b) a space (where a long knot would otherwise be found) followed by a figure-eight knot. To clarify this alternative between a long knot and a figure-eight knot, I note that khipu numbers were normally registered as *completed counts* broken down into their constituent decimal-based units. For instance, in recording the number 115, a pendant string will normally hold one single knot in the 100s position, a second single knot, registering 10, and a long knot registering 5. The point here is that the number 5 would not be registered in the additive form of a long knot of four turns *plus* a figure-eight knot (i.e., $4 + 1 = 5$). Therefore, the long knot and the figure-eight knot are normally *mutually exclusive;* there is usually only one or the other of these knots on a pendant string.

It merits stressing that for the long-knot "type," which is made by turning/twisting the lower (free) end of a string around the upper body of the string 2–9 times, there are *eight* subtypes of this particular knot type that may be constructed. Curiously, although we know the names in Quechua of the cardinal and ordinal numbers that are designated by these various knots, we do not know (to the best of my knowledge) what the names of these three types of knots themselves were in the Quechua language.

Now, when we diagram the three major knot types (as in Figure 4.1), focusing in particular on the principle of pairing (i.e., *ch'ulla/ch'ullantin*) and its relationship to the recording of numbers by means of the succession of different knot types, we recognize that long knots and single knots are employed to signify successive levels, or higher forms, of the achievement of states of "evenness," or *ch'ullantin;* that is, the first long-knot subtype—a long knot of only *two* turns—represents the state of *ch'ullantin* that is formed by the combination of *one* (= a figure-eight knot) and its pair, *two;* further along in the number series, the first appearance of a *single knot* (= 10) represents another (higher) state of *ch'ullantin,* but now, one achieved in the linkage between a long knot of value 9 and a single knot valued 10. Although *five* is not signed by a unique knot *type* (e.g., as in Maya number signing), the long-knot sign for this all-important unit in Quechua numerical organization stands at the midpoint of the group beginning with the figure-eight knot (= 1) and culminating with the first single knot (= 10).

Two important principles can be taken from the above discussion: first, every number that can be spoken or tied into a khipu is either odd (*ch'ulla*) or even (*ch'ullantin*), and second, movement through the three knot types from lowest value (figure-eight) to the next highest knot-type value (long knot) to the highest value (single knot) is signaled by attaining successively higher expressions of pairing (*ch'ullantin*). The first of these statements, however, would seem to leave us with a curious circumstance, particularly if Quechua were to assign numbers to the categories "odd" and "even" in the same way that we do in English or in Spanish and other Romance languages. That is, in Western numbering systems, all complete decimal values—such as 10, 20, 100, 700, 2,000— are classified as even. If the Quechua *were* to construct and value the categories *ch'ulla/ch'ullantin* as we do odd and even, then the numbers 2, 4, 6, and 8, as well as *every* single (i.e., overhand) knot on a khipu— that is, *all* values tied into khipu pendant strings above the units level— would be classified as even. This would suggest an extraordinarily limited relevance for the category odd; in this case, odd (*ch'ulla*) would be limited to the units values 1, 3, 5, 7, and 9.

The issue raised above is important for the argument I am making here because if the "signifying unit" of khipu binary coding is the individual knot rather than the total combined numerical value of all knots on a pendant string, and if only a small percentage of knot values were in fact classified as odd and *none* of the single knots was so classified, this would render the component (i.e., the "bit") of binary coding linked to number values somewhat spurious—that is, the vast majority of binary "bits" coded for number would be classified as even (*ch'ullantin*).

The resolution of the potential asymmetry between the magnitude of the class of odd (*ch'ulla*) numbers as opposed to that of even (*ch'ullantin*) numbers is illustrated in Figure 4.2, which is drawn on the basis of my earlier research on Quechua numeration (see Urton 1997).

In Figure 4.2, we see that in Quechua, the complementary categories of *ch'ulla/ch'ullantin* in fact run through the entire number series,

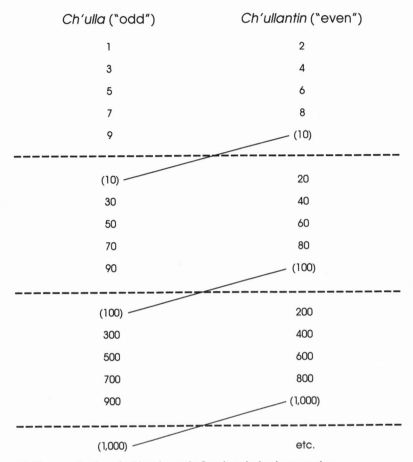

4.2. **The organization of odd and even in Quechua decimal numeration.**

so that, for instance, each of the sets 3 and 4, 30 and 40, 300 and 400, and so on represents a *ch'ulla/ch'ullantin* pair. A cursory look at Figure 4.2 makes it evident that there is a particular problem in designating odd/even values, and in transferring those values to the khipu, which is presented by the full decimal units 10, 100, 1,000, and 10,000. The problem is this: Should these numbers, when tied into a pendant string, be understood as the even partner of the next lowest number (respectively: 9, 99, 999, 9,999)? Or should they be understood to have the status of the odd partner of the next higher number—that is, within the next higher decimal set of which these numbers would represent the lowest member (respectively: 20, 200, 2,000, and 20,000)?

The solution that I propose to the problem outlined above in the

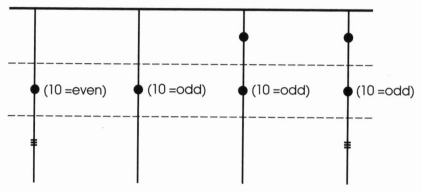

4.3. Proposed rules for assigning odd/even value to single knots.

khipu coding system is as follows: (a) if one of the numbers under discussion (e.g., 10) has some value knotted on the string on a lower level
(in this case: 1–9), and no value stands above it, then the number in
question should be understood as the complement of the lower number and it will, therefore, be coded as even; (b) if the number (e.g., 10)
has *no* number knotted below it, or if there is some other value knotted
on the same or higher level, the 10 will be valued as odd. These particular rules, which I will adopt for coding the khipu, are illustrated in
Figure 4.3. These rules, or principles, will become critical as we proceed
and especially when we set about actually coding a khipu (Chapter 5).

The question that arises now is: How will the principles of classifying
numbers illustrated in Figures 4.2 and 4.3 be reflected in the binary-
coding classifications of knots on pendant strings? I have illustrated
what I think is the answer to this question in a segment of a hypothetical
khipu in Figure 4.4.

Figure 4.4 shows three pendant strings (A, B, and C) registering
three different numerical values. Pendant A registers a figure-eight knot,
which has a value of 1 and is, therefore, odd. Pendant B holds a long knot
of two turns and thus is even. Pendant C registers the total odd number value of 3,433. The question is, how will the knots on Pendant C,
as individual "signifying units," be valued in their binary-coded reading with respect to the binary bit that selects for odd/even? As outlined
earlier, the alternate single knots at each place value (i.e., 10s, 100s, and
1,000s) on Pendant C should be valued as alternately odd and even. To
begin at the bottom of Pendant C, the single long knot of three turns

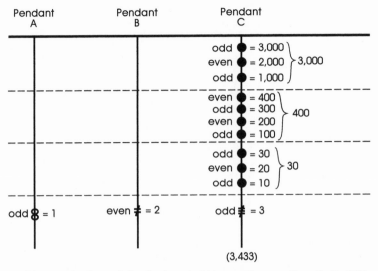

4.4. The organization and distribution of odd/even values on a hypothetical khipu.

will, obviously, be valued odd. Moving up the string to the 10s position, this series of knots will begin with the odd value of 10 followed by the even value of 20 and then the odd value of 30. This pattern of alternating odd and even will obtain at each ascending level of the decimal-place value system.

I would highlight here one characteristic of a few of the khipu with pendant strings bearing multiple single knots in the 10s, 100s, 1,000s, or 10,000s positions that lends support to the suggestion made above that in the binary reading of such series, the knots should be read as having *individual,* alternating odd/even sign values (i.e., rather than the *total* pendant value being assigned a single, unified even or odd value). In the total corpus of khipu that I have studied, there are some fifteen to twenty samples in which the knots of multi-single-knot groupings are tied in different directions (S-knots vs. Z-knots), resulting in arrangements such as those shown in Figure 4.5. In this figure, which is drawn on the basis of data from a khipu in the collection in Chachapoyas, we see on Pendant No. 5, for instance, that the knots in the 1,000s position are tied, from top to bottom, as follows: ZSZZS; in the 100s position, they are tied as follows: ZSZS. Such arrangements as these would support the idea that each knot in such multi-knot series was conceived of as an independent entity.

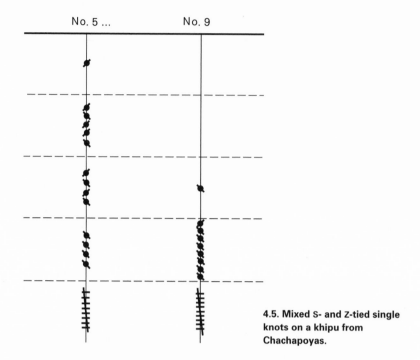

4.5. Mixed S- and Z-tied single knots on a khipu from Chachapoyas.

Before concluding this discussion, I want to emphasize that I believe such knot groupings as those illustrated in Figure 4.5 could always potentially be given *two* different readings. One reading would have been knot by knot, as each knot was evaluated for its particular binary-coded reading, or decoding. The other reading would have been in terms of the value of all knots on that pendant string when read as a full, collective value. This means that, in the hypothesis I am developing here, every knot of a decimal-registry khipu could be read as: (a) an individual binary-coded signifying unit, and (b) a component of a sum that could have been of administrative, calendrical, or even pure mathematical value for state record keepers.

In summary, the system of signing numbers on the khipu was compatible, in terms of its distinctive recording units and their placement, with the organizational principles and structural relations of Quechua numeration in general; the fundamental organizing principle of both Quechua numeration and khipu numerical recording techniques was the *binary* relationship odd/even (*ch'ulla/ch'ullantin*). On these grounds, I argue that there was a fundamental compatibility and complementarity between the cotton/wool, S/Z, and recto/verso binary construction operations discussed in Chapter 3 and the *ch'ulla/ch'ullantin* binary organization of numerical registry in the khipu described in this section.

Decimal and Nondecimal Khipu

At the beginning of this exposition, I indicated that when one studies the arrangement of knots in any given collection of khipu, about two-thirds of the samples will have their knots tied as I have outlined in the previous section; that is, the knot types and their distribution along the length of khipu strings will reflect the hierarchical organization of decimal numerical registration. The guiding principle of the organization of knots by the decimal system of numeration is the same as in our own (decimal) system: any place can hold up to nine units (e.g., 99), any value beyond which one moves to the next higher place value (99 + 1 = 100). Garcilaso de la Vega states this same principle as follows:

> The knots were arranged in order of units, tens, hundreds, thousands, tens of thousands, and seldom if ever passed a hundred thousand, since as each village kept its own records, and each capital the records of its districts, the numbers never in either case went beyond a hundred thousand, though below that figure they made many calculations. . . . These numbers were reckoned by means of knots in the threads, each number being divided from the next. But the knots representing each number were made in a group together, on a loop, like the knots found in the cord of our blessed patriarch St. Francis: this was not difficult to do, as there were never more than nine, seeing that units, tens, etc., never exceed nine. (1966: 330)

The knots referred to by Garcilaso as knots found in the "cord of our blessed patriarch St. Francis" are those described herein as long knots.

Aside from the two-thirds or so of khipu that record decimal values, the remaining one-third of the samples have knot arrangements that, to varying degrees and in different ways, diverge significantly from the regular decimal recording methods described above. For instance, such "nondecimal"—or what I also refer to as "anomalous"—khipu may have pendant strings containing long knots (i.e., the indicators of the units 2–9) that are tied *above* single knots (i.e., the markers of powers of ten). In addition, one can find long knots that are composed of anywhere

from ten to sixteen turns; the latter knot configurations violate the decimal rule governing long knots that when indicating a value greater than
nine, the long knot should be replaced by a single knot in the tens position. Such arrangements and configurations of the three types of knots
as those mentioned here would be comparable to our writing the number 921, but then stating that the 9 should be read in the tens position, the 2 should be read in the ones position, and the 1 should be read
as 100!

Knot Registration and Organization on Anomalous Khipu

Khipu or segments thereof of the type I have referred to as anomalous may have been constructed as registries of narrative rather than
numerical-statistical information (see the discussion of a few examples
of non-numerical khipu in M. Ascher 1986: 282–284). What do such
khipu look like, that is, how are they organized? And how might we go
about understanding their significance and meaning, particularly in relation to the organization of information according to binary coding? I
address these questions in this section.

A segment of an anomalous khipu, a remarkable sample—B/8705
from the American Museum of Natural History—is shown in Figure
4.6.[1] In Figure 4.7, I have illustrated the organization of knots on Pendant Strings Nos. 27–30 of this same khipu; these same pendants are
included within the larger set of pendant strings shown in Table 4.1.
Several pendant strings in Khipu B/8705 carry subsidiary strings, which
I have indicated in Table 4.1 by the designation *s1,* etc. For example,
Pendant No. 25 bears one subsidiary (25s1), which itself bears a subsidiary (25s1s1).

A few words of explanation are in order concerning the transcription system used in Table 4.1. Although I believe that the anomalous
khipu do not primarily register statistical data, nonetheless, since such
khipu do contain various *quantities* of single knots organized in clusters, as well as long knots composed of different *numbers* of turns of
the string within the bodies of the knots, it is most convenient and reasonable to "transcribe" these khipu values using numbers. In the transcription system used in this case, however, each single knot is given the
value 10, regardless of its hierarchical placement on a string. Therefore,
in the transcription used in Table 4.1, there are no higher powers of

TABLE 4.1.
Transcription of Knots on Selected Strings of Khipu B/8705
(AMNH)

Pendant	Transcription (from top of string)
25	40 - 30 - 30
25s1	(7) - (3) - 20
25s1s1	(8) - (6) - 90
26	50 - 30 - 20
26s1	(5) - 70 - 40
27	40 - 50 - 40
28	(4) - 30 - 30
29	(7) - (13) - 30
30	(9) - (12) - 20
30s1	(5) - 20 - 40 - 20
31	1 - 50 - (13)
32	50 - 20 - (12)
33	(7) - (13) - 30
34	(7) - 10 - (5)
34s1	30 - 20 - 60
35	(4) - (10) - 30

ten—such as 100, 1,000, etc.—indicated. In accordance with this registration principle, the transcription of the first pendant string (No. 25)
in Table 4.1 describes a string bearing an arrangement of three clusters
of single knots; beginning at the top of this string (closest to its attachment to the primary cord), there is, first, a cluster of four knots = 40,
then another cluster of three knots = 30, and a final cluster, at the bottom of the string, of three single knots = 30. Thus, the final "reading"
of Pendant No. 25 is: 40-30-30.

As for long knots, the notation convention used in Table 4.1 is to
place a number indicating the number of turns in the long knot in parentheses. For example, a long knot of six turns is transcribed in Table 4.1
as: (6). Thus, the second entry in Table 4, which is a subsidiary string
of Pendant No. 25 (i.e., No. 25s1), contains the following information:
first, a long knot of seven turns = (7), then one of three turns = (3),

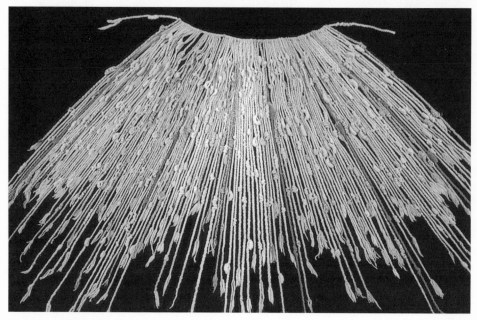

4.6. Khipu B/8705 (AMNH).

and finally, a pair of single knots = 20. As stated earlier and as illustrated in Pendant Subsidiary No. 25s1, we see here that on anomalous khipu, long knots can be found in the highest position on a string, above single knots.

A further comment on the long knots in Khipu B/8705 is in order. On the overwhelming majority of khipu registering decimal values, long knots display a maximum of nine turns, after which—with the addition of one—the long knot will be replaced by a single knot (= 10). However, I have identified long knots on anomalous khipu that contain up to sixteen turns! Therefore, the use of parentheses to enclose long-knot transcriptions will allow us, for instance, to distinguish the notation of a long knot of ten turns = (10) from that of a single single knot = 10. Finally, I would note that in Table 4.1, figure-eight knots are transcribed as 1.

Several features of the organization of knots on the 153 strings (96 pendants + 57 subsidiaries = 153 strings) of Khipu B/8705—which also occur on many other examples of anomalous khipu that I have examined—distinguish these khipu from the majority of samples that appear to have recorded decimal values. Notable among these features is the regular patterning of what I will refer to as "informational units" on

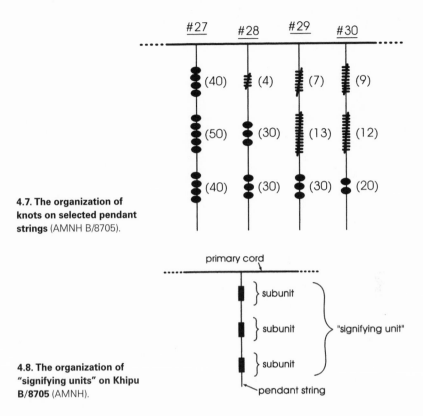

4.7. The organization of knots on selected pendant strings (AMNH B/8705).

4.8. The organization of "signifying units" on Khipu B/8705 (AMNH).

the 153 strings. That is, on 133 of the 153 strings (87%), the information consists of three groups of what I will call notational "subunits"; for example, in the above reading of Pendant No. 25, the three subunits are 40-30-30. I assume that these subunits represent the bits of information on any particular string that go together—in some way that we do not yet understand—to compose what I will refer to as a "signifying unit" (see Figure 4.8). Of the remaining 20 strings, 19 have *four* subunits of information (e.g., see Table 4.1, Pendant No. 30s1); the one remaining string has two subunits of information (this occurs on String No. 70s1s1s1, the subsidiary of the subsidiary of the subsidiary of Pendant No. 70).

What Does a "Signifying Unit" Signify?

The central questions that confront us with respect to khipu such as sample B/8705 (Fig. 4.8) are: What did the "signifying units" signify?

And what was the relationship between that meaning and the reading of the individual knots according to their binary value? I will address the former question first.

One hypothesis that we could propose in answer to the first question above is that these three-subunit signifying units might have represented some form of logograph-like elements. According to such an interpretation, the signifying units might have been like the signs inscribed on early cuneiform tablets, which, as we saw in Chapter 1, were generally composed of names of objects (e.g., agricultural products, state officials, deities, etc.) together with numbers in the system of accounting. In this interpretation, the logographic (word/morpheme level) signifying units would have constituted a type of sign system that Geoffrey Sampson has referred to as a "glottographic" system. In Sampson's scheme, glottographic signing systems are based on signs denoting spoken-language utterances; such signs may take the form of either logograms (e.g., word/morpheme units) or phonograms (e.g., syllabaries, alphabets). Glottographic scripts are distinguished from "semasiographic" sign units, which are nonlanguage utterance-based meaning signs (Sampson 1985: 29–33). To repeat, I suggest herein that the signifying units of B/8705 may have represented glottographic signs that were assigned conventionalized (nonphonological) word/morpheme-level values by the khipukamayuq.

If various grapheme-based writing systems can arbitrarily ascribe both logographic and phonological values to signs scratched on two-dimensional surfaces, I see no reason in principle why the Inka could not have assigned such values to their anomalous string constructions. In this case, each pendant string, together with its three-set cluster of anomalous knots (in combination with other factors such as color, spin/ply, attachment, and knot-directional variations), could even have held sentence-level utterances. To be clear, I am not arguing here that the anomalous khipu signifying units *did* denote glottographic (whether logographic or phonological) values; however, I maintain strongly that there is no reason, in principle, why the khipukamayuq could *not* have assigned either of these classes of values to their knots should they have chosen to do so. This would mean that the Inka *could* have developed and deployed vocabularies of sign units, which they encoded on khipu like B/8705, in which they "inscribed"—tied, dyed, and twisted—basic information for later retrieval by trained khipukamayuq.

Before moving on to a consideration of colors, we must confront an issue that may already have begun to concern the reader. The issue in question is whether or not the binary reading of khipu knots emphasized earlier in this study is incompatible, and therefore in competition, with the interpretation of anomalous khipu outlined above, as well as with any number of other analyses produced to date that argue for the patterning of information in terms of repetitions of number sequences (e.g., M. Ascher 1986, 1991; Ascher and Ascher 1997; Pereyra 1996), the representation of fractions or ratios (Ascher and Ascher 1997: 143– 151), and arrangements of numbers in calendrically significant patterns (e.g., Nordenskiöld 1925a, 1925b; Urton 2001; Zuidema 1989). As I have suggested above, I see no reason why these two types or modes of reading could not have coexisted. Such a situation, it seems to me, would not have been significantly different from what we find in those script systems in which the "letters" ordinarily employed in signing parts of words were also used as the signs of numerals—e.g., in Greek: $\alpha = 1$, $\beta = 2$, $\gamma = 3$, etc. (Threatte 1996: 279; Waanders 1992). Such script systems also include Georgian (Holisky 1996: 364) and Hebrew (Menninger 1977: 262–267). In such systems, the reading that was to be given to any particular letter sign—that is, whether it was meant to sign a letter of a word or a quantifying adjective (i.e., a number)—depended upon context.

Were the Khipu Signs Iconic?

We have recognized from the beginning of this study that, as a three-dimensional string-and-knot-based recording device, the khipu does not appear (at least not obviously) to have operated on the basis of signing representational, iconic images or values. An example of iconicity from early grapheme-based writing traditions could include, for instance, a picture of a person's head with mouth open to sign the logogram "to speak" or "speaking." Surely we can confidently conclude that the khipu was an aniconic signing system? In general terms, and from what I understand of the system at present, I think this latter characterization of the khipu is probably an accurate representation—certainly there are no characterizations of khipu in the colonial documents (other than the questionable "Naples documents"; see Chapter 1) that would suggest otherwise. Nonetheless, I strongly resist characterizing or classifying the khipu as non- or aniconic. The reason for my hesitancy is that we do not

yet know what the final solution to the puzzle of the khipu will be—
that is, how (if ever) these devices will be decoded and the system de-
ciphered. Until we determine what was readable and how each element
was read, I see no reason to close off any given interpretive approach.

For instance, one can imagine, given the complex arrangements of
the hundreds of three subunits of information of pendants composing
the signifying units of anomalous khipu, as described in the previous
section, that khipukamayuq might have understood (either conceived or
perceived) some particular alignment and configuration of knots with
constituent colors to have formed a "likeness"—an icon—of some object or structure in their world. To make one highly speculative suggestion, I have often mused, in studying the long knots, how much they
resemble the ridge line of the knuckles when the hand is made into a
fist. In this respect, I have wondered if a long knot of four turns (i.e.,
like the four knuckles of the fist) could have been "read," iconically, as
an image of the hand, and been given that (even logographic) value?

Similarly, we might ask the general question of whether or not long
knots, all of which can be read as composed of iterative stroke-like units
between two and nine lines, could have been viewed by khipukamayuq as having had some iconic properties. For example, a long knot
of seven turns could have been read as seven (linear?) objects lined up
side by side. However, values above nine, which are signaled by single
knots, would lose this potential iterative/iconic quality, trading it as they
would for abstract, symbolic denotations. That is, a single knot can represent 10, 20, 100, or whatever full decimal value, but it does not look
like that number of objects (as a long knot does its value).

I see nothing to be gained by speculating further along this particular line of interpretation at the present time. I simply want to establish
for the reader what I consider to be a potentially important ancillary
mode of signing—iconic—that could conceivably have contributed to
the representation and production of meaning in the khipu.

The Binary Organization of Colors

A survey of the khipu specimens in any one of the major museum collections will convince one of the importance of the coding and patterning
of elements by means of color in the khipu recording system (for discussions of the organization and possible significance of colors, see Arellano

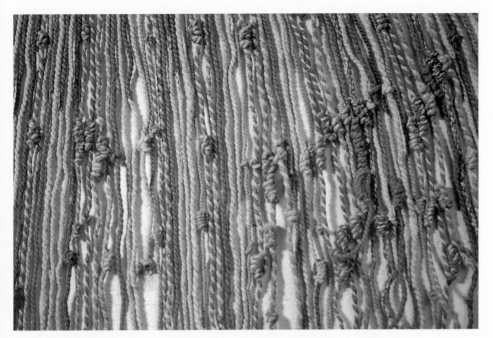

4.9. Khipu with "barber-pole" pendants (Museum für Völkerkunde, Berlin, VA 42554).

1999; Ascher and Ascher 1997; Loza 1998; Pärssinen 1992; Pereyra 1997; and Radicati di Primeglio 1979; for excellent treatments of the symbolism of colors in Andean weavings, see Cereceda 1986, 1990; and Paul 1990). For khipu made of both cotton and camelid fibers, color variation resulted both from the variation of natural hues and from dyeing in a remarkable range of colors (see below).

Individual cotton or woolen strings were spun from yarns of different colors to produce a mottled, multicolored effect, or yarns of two or more distinct colors were plied to produce a "barber-pole" effect (Figure 4.9). Some strings are composed of yarns of different colors spliced together down the length of the string. There are also examples of long knots whose color changes in the middle of the knot (Figure 4.10).

The Aschers have provided valuable analyses of color patterning in the khipu, particularly with regard to the division and organization of groups of pendant strings in complex, rhythmic color patterns (1997: 122–131). In this same vein, the renowned, dedicated, and unfortunately now deceased Peruvian khipu specialist Carlos Radicati di Primeglio (see esp. 1964) argued that close study of the "seriation"—by

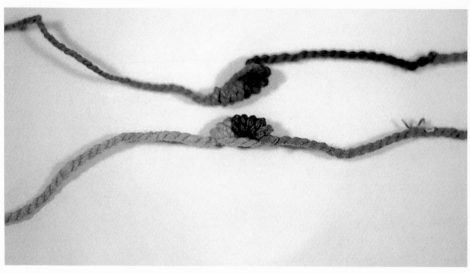

4.10. Color change within long knots (Museum für Völkerkunde, Berlin, VA 47106 A and B).

which he meant repetitive schemes and patterning—of string colors may represent a fruitful approach to deciphering the khipu (Figure 4.11). Although he argued forcefully and creatively for this methodology, Radicati himself did not claim to have made significant breakthroughs in interpreting khipu by this method. Salomon (2002) also found seriation-like organizations of dyed woolen threads in the khipu of Tupicocha.

It is fair to say, I think, that we have made less headway in our attempts to formulate convincing arguments for the possible meaning and symbolism of colors than for perhaps any other component of the khipu recording system. The principal sources of information on the symbolism of colors in the khipu are accounts provided in two of the Spanish chronicles written during the early seventeenth century. Most notably, the famed Garcilaso de la Vega, descendant of Inka nobility on his mother's side and the blood of a conquistador on his father's, claimed deep knowledge of the khipu. Garcilaso gives us to understand that there existed what amounts to a kind of one-to-one correspondence between colors and meanings, ". . . such as yellow for gold, white for silver, and red for warriors" (1966: 330). The Augustinian friar Antonio de la Calancha, who claims to have made a careful, systematic study of khipu recording methods, expanded the inventory of color symbols by pointing out that crimson represented the Inka, black denoted time, and

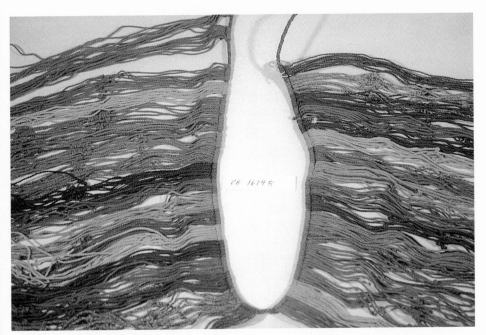

4.11. Color "seriation" of khipu pendant strings (Museum für Völkerkunde, Berlin, VA 16148).

green was used to signify the dead; furthermore, Calancha says that each province in the empire had its own khipu signifier in the form of strings and knots of a certain configuration and combination of colors (Calancha 1974 [1638], 1:206; see Pärssinen [1992: 38–41] for suggestions as to how these provincial signifiers may have been formed).

Now, it may well have been the case that the khipu information system *did*, in fact, employ colors as symbolic (i.e., signifying) elements in the kind of one-to-one system of correspondences described by Garcilaso and Calancha. If so, then our task in this regard is merely one of combing the colonial documents, dictionaries, and chronicles as carefully as possible in order to identify all correspondences between color and meaning described therein. I, however, have grave doubts about Garcilaso's and Calancha's versions of the way color was supposedly used to sign meaning; at least I question the degree to which these accounts provide us with anything like the full and complete story on the symbolic significance of colors in the khipu. There are two reasons for my reservations. First (and perhaps least compelling to the reader), the system as described by the two chroniclers is too simplistic and—finally—Western. As anyone who has spent any time studying the Inka knows, virtually *nothing* in their habits or ways of doing things ever seems to have had a simple, formulaic pattern, as suggested by Garcilaso de la Vega and Calancha for colors in the khipu. Certainly there is no case (that I am aware of) in which meaning appears to have been construed in neat, one-to-one symbol "packages," as has been suggested for khipu color symbolism.

Second, and most compelling in my view, is the point that *if* the one-to-one signing of meanings with colors described by Garcilaso and Calancha *was* indeed the full extent of the matter, then this should cause us to question profoundly the salience of Ascher and Ascher's notion of "insistence," discussed in Chapter 2. That is, if we find that in virtually every other domain of life and culture that the Inka manner of classification and organization was to establish dual or binary—and in certain contexts triadic, quadripartite, quinary, and decimal—categories and relations between elements, why would they have suddenly abandoned these powerful and persistent classificatory, organizational, and semantic strategies when they set about ordering relations between, and assigning meaning to, colors? I do not think they would have done that, nor do I believe they did so.

As a theoretical and analytical point of departure, I will adopt the position that "insistence" *is,* in fact, a valid assumption for us to make regarding the nature of knowledge and practice in all domains of the life and culture of any (at least pre-postmodern) society and that, therefore, accounts of color symbolism like those given by Garcilaso and Calancha probably provide us with only a part, or a superficial version, of the total picture. The question is, however, where do we locate a model for conceptualizing the organization and meaning of colors in the Inka khipu that is consistent with the powerful principle of binary organization employed in every other aspect of the construction of these devices?

Concerning the possible binary conception and organization of colors used in dyed khipu strings, the most interesting (and in fact the only) model that I am aware of is a tradition of color classification in use today among weavers throughout central Bolivia, especially in the region of Tarabuco and Candelaria (see Dávalos, Cereceda, and Martínez 1994: 25–26). I became familiar with this system in 1993–1994 while carrying out field research on Quechua numbers and mathematics, during which time I apprenticed myself to master weavers in the village of

4.12. María Condori, master dyer and weaver from Candelaria.

Candelaria (see Urton 1997). The Quechua-speaking weavers in Candelaria and Tarabuco organize the process of dyeing yarn, and they segregate the differently colored threads in their weavings into two broad color groupings or categories (Figure 4.12). The master weavers in these villages, who are called Mamas (Mothers), refer to these two color groupings as *k'uychi* (rainbow).

One of the *k'uychi* groupings is commonly called Puka K'uychi (Red Rainbow). I have also heard this color grouping referred to as Kamaq K'uychi; the term "Kamaq" may be glossed generally as "Creator,"

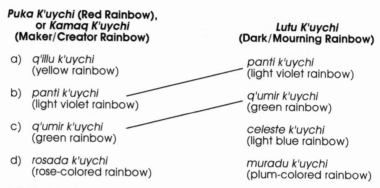

**Puka K'uychi (Red Rainbow),
or Kamaq K'uychi
(Maker/Creator Rainbow)**

**Lutu K'uychi
(Dark/Mourning Rainbow)**

a) q'illu k'uychi
    (yellow rainbow)

panti k'uychi
(light violet rainbow)

b) panti k'uychi
    (light violet rainbow)

q'umir k'uychi
(green rainbow)

c) q'umir k'uychi
    (green rainbow)

celeste k'uychi
(light blue rainbow)

d) rosada k'uychi
    (rose-colored rainbow)

muradu k'uychi
(plum-colored rainbow)

4.13. The *k'uychi* and sub-*k'uychi* of the Tarabuco-Candelaria region.

"Maker," or, as Taylor suggests, "Organizer"; "Animator" (1976: 233–236). The other major color category is called Lutu K'uychi, which may be translated as "Dark," or "Mourning Rainbow." These two major color categories are each subdivided into four subgroupings of colors; the subgroupings are also referred to as *k'uychi*. Two of these minor, or what I will call sub-, *k'uychi* are shared between the two major color groupings so that there are, in fact, a total of only six (not eight) unique sub-*k'uychi* (see Figure 4.13).

The two main *k'uychi* classes represent what we could call major thematic color groupings, whereas the sub-*k'uychi* represent the minor thematic color groupings *into* which the major groupings may be divided or *from* which they are formed. As I have noted, there is no categorical name differentiation between the major and minor rainbows; both are termed *k'uychi*. However, a listener will know to what level of rainbow any given reference is being made, because the term *k'uychi* will generally be preceded by a color term; if that term is either *puka* or *kamaq*, on the one hand, or *lutu*, on the other, the listener will know that reference is being made to one or the other of the major color classes. Reference to any one of the minor hues will be signaled by a specific sub-*k'uychi* color term.

As for the actual organization of hues within the six sub-*k'uychi*, each contains a series of graded shadings of the particular color hue in question (see below). Textiles composed of one or the other of the sub-*k'uychi* of the Puka/Kamaq K'uychi grouping have an overall reddish yellowish tint, and those composed of a sub-*k'uychi* within the

Lutu K'uychi grouping have a bluish purplish tint. Light violet and green (*panti k'uychi* and *q'umir k'uychi,* respectively) are shared between the two major color groupings. In sum, at a general level, we find in these data an overall binary organization of colors used by the weavers of this region of central Bolivia; that is, any given textile will generally be composed of threads of *either* Puka/Kamaq K'uychi *or* Lutu K'uychi.

Depending on the informant with whom one discusses this organization of colors, the six different sub-*k'uychi* are composed of from four to six shades of the dominant color of the sub-*k'uychi* in question (e.g., compare the color terms in Figure 4.13 with those in Dávalos, Cereceda, and Martínez 1994: 26). The shading and intensity of colors within each sub-*k'uychi* follow the same general scheme; this was described to me by one woman in Candelaria for the sub-*k'uychi* called *q'umir k'uychi* (green rainbow) as follows:

t'uqran	pale [green]
qhipan	next [darker green]
qhipan	next [darker green]
maman	mother [darkest green]
(*tatan*	father [black])

The sequence goes from the lightest shade of green (*t'uqran*) to the darkest (*maman*). On first glance, threads dyed in *maman* (mother), the darkest shade of the color in question (in this case, green), often appear to be *black;* however, on closer inspection, it will always be seen that the "black" has a particular faint tint, which indicates its relationship, or "kinship," to one or the other of the sub-*k'uychi*. It is important to note that certain of the master weavers of the Tarabuco area say that most of the sub-*k'uychi* also contain one additional "color" beyond "*maman*"; this color is *yana* (black/dark), which is referred to—in the kinship model of color shading—as *tatan,* or "father." The use of kinship terms in describing color categories and relations is crucial in helping us to understand how color shades and intensities are considered to be related to each other. In particular, these terms introduce the principles of hierarchy based on age and, to a lesser degree, gender into the organization of color.

Binary Organization of Natural Color Hues

It is critical to point out that whereas the model developed above for binary color coding in the khipu derives from the color terminologies and symbolism of dyes and dyed fabrics among present-day central Bolivian weavers, a large proportion of the colors of ancient khipu were, in fact, the natural color differences of cotton and wool. As for cotton, pre-Hispanic coastal Peruvian populations produced cotton in a tremendous variety of colors: white, beige, light brown, medium brown, dark brown, chocolate, reddish, orange brown, and mauve (Conklin 2002). The majority of cotton-based khipu from coastal sites display a range of these natural hues, either as the single hue of a one-color khipu or spun and plied in mottled, barber-pole, and other multihued color arrays. In addition to cotton, camelid fibers were available in an equally broad variety of colors, from black through numerous and subtle shades of grays, rust reds, browns, and almost pure white (Flores Ochoa 1986; Molina 1916: 25).

I would hypothesize that there was a binary organization of these natural (cotton and wool fiber) hues that would have been structurally and symbolically compatible, or homologous, with the two rainbow groupings of dyed khipu colors. The suggestion that I would make most confidently at present would be that the binary opposition between the Red/Creator Rainbow and the Dark/Mourning Rainbow can be seen in the opposition between light and dark that occurs naturally for wool and cotton fibers. In such a model, the rusts, grays, and browns would have fallen between the two head categories in a manner that I am not able to reconstruct with any certainty at this time.

The above hypothesis for the binary organization of cotton and wool colors does find some modest support in one of the few studies we have of the use and community curatorship of khipu in the Andes today; this is in the village of Tupicocha, studied by Frank Salomon (2002). Salomon was told by a person who is skilled and knowledgeable in dyeing, weaving, and knitting that the Tupicochan khipu are divided into two color categories: dark and light. This "color" pairing organizes the ten community-held khipu into two sets whose colors include both natural and dyed hues (Salomon, personal communication 2001).

The Complementary Binary Organization of Numbers and Colors

I would argue, from the material presented in this chapter, that there was a coincidence between the binary coding of numbers and colors in the Inka khipu. My hypothesis in this regard, as constructed on an analogy with the conceptualization and organization of numbers and colors among central Bolivian Quechua-speaking weavers today, is that colors were conceptualized and organized into two groupings: Puka/ Kamaq K'uychi and Lutu K'uychi for dyed threads, on the one hand, and light and dark for naturally hued cotton and wool fibers, on the other. These binary color classes would have been structurally (i.e., syntactically) and perhaps semantically related to the binary and complementary *ch'ulla/ch'ullantin* (odd/even) organization of numbers in the khipu number-registration system. In addition, I suggest that the four-to-six-part shading of hues within the sub-*k'uychi* groupings would have been structurally equivalent and perhaps semantically complementary to the second-level, quinary principle of the organization of Quechua numbers that I have described and analyzed in my study of Quechua numerical ontology and ethnomathematics (Urton 1997). In that system, numbers are organized in terms of five-part "family" groupings of a mother and her four age-graded offspring.

I would conclude by noting that I do not think the binary system of color classifications found in central Bolivia that is outlined above is necessarily incompatible with what Garcilaso and Calancha report concerning colors. However, in order to link the two "systems," we would have to accept that any given color, along with its symbolism (e.g., as given by the chroniclers), would have been seen in complementary opposition to some other color and its symbolism. The two colors would have formed a complete (i.e., *ch'ullantin*) binary pair of colors and meanings.

With the descriptions and analyses provided in Chapters 3 and 4, we have now arrived at a comprehensive understanding of the universe of operations and classifications that produced the seven-bit binary sequences of the "code of the khipu." In the next chapter, we will attempt to put this system into operation in order to understand, in terms of practical strategies and operations of encoding and decoding, just how these complex recording devices were manipulated in the storage and retrieval of different types of information.

CHAPTER 5

Khipu Sign Capacity and Code Conversion

Having provided an overview of the basic structural properties and the physical and linguistic features of the (hypothetical) binary coding system of the khipu, I now address two important issues of a more pragmatic nature. The first question concerns the information storage capacity of this coding system (Figure 5.1). How much information could the khipu encode? Phrased another way, how many unique signs could be produced from the potential variation of characters composing the seven-bit knots? Was the storage capacity of khipu sufficient to accommodate the distinctions characteristic of, for instance, logographic, syllabic, logosyllabic, and other types of signing systems? The second question concerns the likely sequence of tasks that would have been followed by a khipukamayuq in first encoding and then decoding, or reading, one of these devices. We will find later in this chapter that, at least in certain circumstances or for the reading of certain types of khipu, the information in the khipu was brought into relationship—that is, it was "interfaced"—with configurations or arrays of stones, beads, or other forms of counters.

How Much Information Could a Khipu Hold?

As I stated in Chapter 2, the theory of khipu recording and reading I am developing herein is premised on the notion that the base coding or signifying unit was a seven-bit binary array.[1] Now, in the khipu binary coding system whose various elements we have defined in Chapters 3 and 4, if each bit of information composing the proposed seven-bit sequences had only two options, this would result in a coding system that could have recorded 128 distinct information units (2 to the 7th = 128). We will leave to the side for the moment the question of the

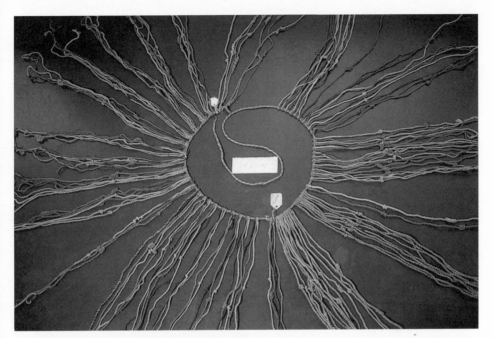

5.1. Khipu (Museum für Völkerkunde, Berlin, VA 63040).

nature of the "information units" signed by these seven-bit sequences (e.g., were they codes for logograms? logosyllabograms?) and return to this problem later.

In fact, the system that we have elaborated to this point would have actually had a far greater storage capacity than the 128 possible signs, or characters, derived above. This is because of the greater number of identities that could fill the color bit, or slot, in the seven-bit coded sequences. In the description of the system of color coding that I hypothesized in Chapter 4, we saw that there were six distinct classes ("sub-*k'uychi*") of colors, each of which was composed of a minimum of four shades of a given hue; this results in a color-bit coding component made up of 24 different, named colors. Another way to describe this array and organization of color hues is to note that there were eight *distinct* colors within each of the two main *k'uychi* groupings (= 16 colors), with an additional eight colors that were shared between the two main *k'uychi* classes, which results in an inventory of twenty-four colors (16 + 8 = 24; see Figure 4.13).

Now, color was one of the seven bits of information in any given binary-coded sequence in the khipu; thus, in a fully coded signifying unit (a knot), six bits would have been accounted for by the binary construction features of the knot (including its numerical value) and the string into which it was tied. The remaining one bit would have been filled by one of the twenty-four different possible color identities. This arrangement would result in seven-bit patterns that could code for 1,536 distinct information units; that is: (2 to the 6th) = 64 × 24 = 1,536. Finally, I must note that this number would have been even greater in the case of knots that were tied into multicolored strings, or knots whose color changed within the body of the knot. I will leave this additional signing capacity to the side for the present time.

It is difficult to know precisely how to factor into the above equations the bit in a binary-coded array that would have been linked to number. We learned in Chapter 4 that, in general terms, any given number was (and still is, in Quechua today) valued as either odd (*ch'ulla*) or even (*ch'ullantin*). Now, if the bit of information in the seven-bit coded arrays that was linked to number was valued *only* as either odd or even, regardless of what the particular number might happen to be, then the number bit of khipu coding would itself remain a binary factor and this would not disturb the estimate of 1,536 different possible units of information arrived at above. If, however, we were to say that there were as many distinct codes for the characters that could occupy either the *ch'ulla* (odd) or *ch'ullantin* (even) identity of a coded number bit as there are even and odd numbers, this would obviously result in a theoretically infinite number of possible distinctive seven-bit arrays in the khipu.

I will argue here for the more conservative of the two principles outlined above for valuing the one bit of information in khipu coding that coded for number. That is, I think it most likely that the slot, or bit, of a seven-bit coded khipu array that signed number would only have been *either ch'ulla or ch'ullantin* (odd or even, respectively), regardless of what the actual number—that is, how great its magnitude—was. Beyond this, however, I argue that the actual quantitative difference between any two values—for instance, the difference between the odd-number values 3 and 5—situated within binary arrays that were identical in all other respects (i.e., in terms of the qualities of the other six bits of the seven-bit arrays) would represent different "types" of the same "class": for instance, different species of the same genus. As an example to illustrate this last point, let us say that a particular seven-bit array whose number-bit value was coded odd (*ch'ulla*) represented the sign or marker for "bird," or winged/flying creature. In such a circumstance, the version of this array represented by the actual odd number 3 might have referred to a *kuntur* (condor), whereas the "bird" sign containing an odd value of 5 might denote a *waman* (falcon). According to the conservative interpretation advanced here, then, the total inventory of distinctive sign units of the khipu binary coding system would be preserved at 1,536, as calculated earlier.

The question that we should address now is: Where does the derived number of distinctive coding units (1,536) leave us in terms of the question of the type of signing system that could have been handled by a coding system of this magnitude? For comparative purposes, we may note that the various alphabetic systems used in the different ancient and modern writing systems of the Western world have utilized between twenty and thirty recurring signs, a range of signs that is far below what could have been accommodated by the khipu recording system. As for syllabaries, the Mycenaean Linear B script used some eighty-eight signs, and the Cherokee syllabic script invented by Sequoyah (ca. 1770–1843) contains eighty-five characters (Scancarelli 1996: 587). In general, syllabaries tend to have between fifty and ninety signs (Coulmas 1992: 42). Again, such a number could easily have been accommodated by the khipu signing system, as theorized herein. But what about the remaining sign units? Surely if the Inka devised a coding system that could have comfortably accommodated 1,536 distinct coded units, they would not have created and maintained such a rich system in order to sign only some fifty to ninety signs. So, what type of signing system calls for the approximate number of seven-bit coding characters that were actually available in the khipu system?

When we turn to the ancient scripts of the Near East, we find, for instance, that the early, pre-phoneticized Sumerian cuneiform script used between 1,000 and 1,500 logographic signs; this number was reduced to some 600 logosyllabic signs as the script became heavily phoneticized (Cooper 1996: 41; Gragg 1996: 68; Nissen, Damerow, and Englund 1993: 117). As for Chinese, the earliest scripts of the Shang period used about 4,500 characters, although only about 1,000 have been identified to date (DeFrancis 1989: 96–99).[2] Victor Mair notes that the command of approximately 2,400 diverse signs is considered essential for basic reading and writing skills in modern Chinese (1996: 200), and Florian Coulmas has noted that in publications in present-day China, about 90 percent of the content is signed by roughly 1,000 characters (1992: 100). And finally, after estimating the total sign inventory of Maya writing at around 750 signs, J. Eric Thompson gave the following comparative summary: "In comparison with this total of 750 Maya signs, the total of Egyptian symbols excluding ligatures and numbers is 604, and the hieroglyphic symbols listed in Gardiner's *Egyptian Grammar* reach 734 . . ." (1991 [1962]: 19). These estimates are consistent with the figure of 700 signs given by Robert Ritner (1996: 74) for the number of Egyptian hieroglyphs used during the Middle Egyptian period (ca. 2000–1650 B.C.E.) and Michael Coe and Mark van Stone's figure of 800 signs for Mayan (2001: 19). The Mayan and Egyptian hieroglyphic writing systems were both based on logosyllabic signs (with the addition of determinatives, number signs, etc.).

The point of the above very sketchy set of figures on the size of sign inventories in different types of script systems is that, with its 1,536 possible binary-coded arrays, the coding system of the khipu would have had the potential to encode a full complement of most of the sign inventories characterizing the writing systems of many ancient civilizations, including logograms, syllabograms, and logosyllabograms. If we can draw any reasonable inference from this discussion, I would say it would be that the khipu binary coding system would have been most comparable, in terms of its information storage capacity, to an unphoneticized logographic or a mixed logosyllabographic signing system—a system similar to early cuneiform, Chinese (Shang), and Egyptian and Mayan hieroglyphic scripts.

Encoding and Decoding a Khipu Text

We turn next to the question of how khipu were made and read. I note to begin with that we do not have explicit testimony from the colonial documents or chronicles of precisely how these objects were read or of how the technological and intellectual traditions and the memory-based elements of the system were brought into relationship with each other in the encoding and decoding of any given khipu. What can be said with regard to these traditions and procedures represents a construction—in fact a deduction—from close study of the physical features of the khipu themselves (e.g., see Conklin 2002), augmented by analogies that represent inferences from ethnographic fieldwork on contemporary Andean intellectual and symbolic traditions that, I believe, are relevant for the reconstruction of those same traditions as they informed the Inka khipu. My basic argument is that the khipu was a product of, and a device designed for, binary coding. Some components of this system were binary by necessity, we might say, in the sense that they were the results of manipulating strings in three-dimensional space. Other elements (e.g., numbers and colors) were binary by attribution—that is, as a part of symbolic constructions and general linguistic semiosis.

A model showing the connection between the binary organization of information and the hierarchy of binary decision making and string manipulations in the khipu is presented in Figure 5.2.

Beginning at the top of Figure 5.2 (Level I) and moving to the bottom (Level VII), this figure diagrams the sequence of decision-making events and string-manipulation procedures that I think would have been followed in the construction of any given khipu. At the beginning of the process of constructing either a numerical-statistical or a narrative khipu, a decision would have been made with regard to the type of material that was to be used in the construction of each string of the khipu. Would the strings be spun from cotton or camelid fiber (wool)? Once the material was selected, the decision that faced the khipukamayuq was: From what color class would the dye applied to a given string be drawn: Red/Creator Rainbow or Dark Rainbow? Or, if the string was composed of wool or cotton and the khipukamayuq wanted to leave the material its natural color, what would its color class be?

Once the above decisions had been made and the relevant tasks executed, the process of constructing and assembling the khipu would begin. This was the process of actually registering the information—"writing the text"—according to a particular syntactical framework or format (see M. Ascher 2002 on khipu formats). The beginning of this process was marked by the khipukamayuq's construction of a primary cord, which would be composed of dyed threads spun and plied either Z/S or S/Z, as well as (if the maker chose to do so) the addition of a wrapping in S or Z. It is likely that the appearance of the primary cord would have given some indication of the subject matter of the khipu. What we await, and desperately need, is a full inventory of the primary cords of

Level	Information	Decision/ Operation
I	material	cotton/wool ○ ●
II	color class	Red Rainbow/ Dark Rainbow ○ ●
III	spin/ply	Z/S / S/Z ○ ●
IV	pendant attachment	recto/verso ○ ●
V	knot directionality	Z/S ○ ●
VI	number class	*ch'ulla/* *ch'ullantin* ○ ●
VII	information type	decimal/ nondecimal ○ ●

○ White stone

● Black stone

5.2. Forms and levels of binary-coded elements in the khipu.

the 600 or so extant khipu. Such an inventory could be extremely helpful to us in establishing a possible khipu typology.

The khipukamayuq would then set about constructing the khipu strings. This process required deciding on the spin and ply pattern of each string; would any given string be S-spun/Z-plied or Z-spun/S-plied? The completed strings would then be attached to the primary cord in either the recto or the verso fashion, taking into account any spacing between strings or groups of strings that the khipukamayuq might have wanted to maintain as a way of classifying the information in the khipu. Once the requisite number of strings had been appended to the primary cord and the appropriate top strings and subsidiary strings added, the pendant strings would then be knotted.

Depending on whether the message to be encoded into a given string was statistical or narrative, the knots would be constructed, respectively, in accordance with the hierarchical place notation system of Quechua decimal numeration or in accordance with (nondecimal) "anomalous" knotting conventions in which semantic values might have been assigned to knot types and knot clusters in arbitrary (i.e., culturally determined) conventional attributions. In actually tying each knot, the khipukamayuq decided what was the appropriate knotting type: S or Z. In terms of the timing of the knotting of the strings, it seems to me most reasonable to think that the strings would have been knotted *after* they were tied onto the primary cords, because, at least in the case of the decimal khipu, this would have made it easier for the khipukamayuq to tie the knots in their appropriate place value. I suppose it would have been possible to knot the strings of nondecimal (i.e., narrative) khipu before attaching them to the primary cord.

I would stress that, except for the choice of individual color hue (though this *was* true of the overall color class), every operation described above was a result of binary decision making.

Did "Khipu makers" (Khipukamayuq) Actually Make the Khipu?

I should say a few words here concerning what we know about who actually constructed these devices. That is, who sheared the wool and carded the cotton? Who spun and plied the raw fibers into strings? And who dyed, attached, and then knotted the strings? To the best of my knowledge, we do not have any explicit accounts in the literature produced by Spanish colonial administrators that supply us with answers to these questions. Not even Garcilaso de la Vega, who claimed considerable knowledge of the khipu (see Urton 2002; Zamora 1988), says anything about who actually made the khipu. The nearest we get to commentary on this matter is in the chronicle of the seventeenth-century Augustinian friar Antonio de la Calancha.

In his chronicle entitled *Crónica moralizada del orden de San Agustín en el Perú* (1974, 1:201–208), Calancha gives an extensive discussion of what he learned about khipu from his personal investigations. His commentary includes information on the symbolism of colors, the manner of indicating place-names in the khipu, ways of signifying time, and other interesting and important topics. For example, he says that a crimson thread spun into a string signified the Inka king, as this color was used only by and for royalty. He adds that in order to signify that the Inka had subdued ten provinces, a khipu would bear a brown (*pardo*) string having ten knots tied into it.

While supplying us with valuable and unique information, the latter testimony also points up the problematical nature of Calancha's account, for, as we have seen above and as is attested to specifically by Garcilaso de la Vega, a quantity of ten would be signified not by *ten* knots but rather by *one* knot in the tens position. This and a few other similar problems notwithstanding, Calancha does give us some very intriguing and seemingly reliable information in his account of khipu recording and reading. However, on the matter that we are concerned with here—that is, the question of who actually made the khipu—Calancha is not very helpful. For instance, he does not say who made the crimson dye or who spun the crimson-colored thread together with other strings; nor does he say who knotted the brown string to signify the ten provinces captured by the Inka. What Calancha does say regarding the actual activities of the khipukamayuq is the following:

> . . . whether because of the privileges with which they honored the office, or because if they did not give a good accounting concerning that on which they were questioned they would be severely castigated, they [the khipukamayuq] continually studied the signs, ciphers, and relations, teaching them to those who would succeed them in office, and there were many of these Secretaries, each of whom was assigned his particular class of material, having to suit [or fit] the story, tale, or song to the knots of which they served as indices, and points of "site memory" [*punto para memoria local*]. (Calancha 1974: 205; my translation)[3]

Curiously, Calancha's account leaves us with the impression, since he asserts that the khipukamayuq fit the stories to the khipu structures (rather than the reverse), that someone other than the khipu makers might have made the khipu and that it was the khipukamayuq's job to find a way to fit the narrative to the (constructed) khipu. But this may be to read too much into Calancha's account, given that he was interested primarily in questions having to do with writing and memory skills in this passage, not with the—what I imagine for him would have been more mundane—subject matter of who produced the physical components of the khipu themselves.

The fact that we do not have accounts of the processes connected with making the khipu could perhaps be explained by the ubiquity of the performance of the general types of activities involved in making khipu-like (especially textile) constructions in communities throughout the Andes during the colonial era. That is, the various skills and procedures of producing textiles (i.e., cloth) in the Andes are essentially the same as those required in making khipu; these include spinning, plying, dyeing, and knotting threads (e.g., see Guaman Poma's drawing of the *acllaconas* [chosen women] who are engaged in spinning; Figure 5.3). In their everyday intercourse with people in villages, towns, and the newly formed cities (*reducciones*) throughout the Andes, the Spanish conquistadors, priests, and other colonials would have been aware of an enormous and continuous production of textiles. Thus, it may not have struck any one of the colonial commentators on the khipu that an explanation of who actually made these textile recording devices was called for—or perhaps the issue was simply not of much interest to them.

An analogy to the circumstance I am describing here for the Andes— in which many people who were *not* directly involved in producing records nonetheless worked daily with the tools of record keeping— would be a hypothetical circumstance in which in Mesopotamia, for instance, large numbers of people in communities along the Tigris and Euphrates would have spent the better part of every day working with clay tablets and styluses to produce some *nontextual* product side by side with the Sumerian scribes who worked with these same materials inscribing cuneiform signs on clay tablets. This is precisely the situation that obtained in the Andes: many people were working with the materials and skills of weaving (spinning, plying, and knotting threads) in every community, but (presumably) only a few specialists were using those same materials, and probably similar techniques of manipulating threads, in the production of knotted-string statistical and narrative records. It is to be hoped that someday in the future we will encounter documentary evidence that will inform us more precisely on the vitally important topic of who actually made these knotted-string devices.

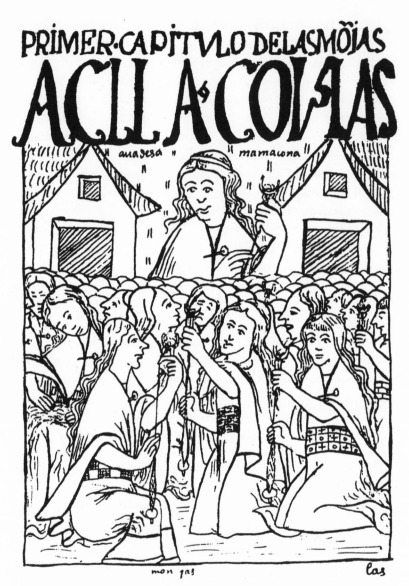

5.3. Virgins of the Sun spinning threads (Guaman Poma 1980 [1615]: 273 [298]).

Upon taking up a khipu to "read" the message encoded therein, a khipukamayuq would have run through a series of visual and tactile queries, "interfacing" knowledge of the standardized values attached to the choices between binary categories that could possibly have been made on each level of construction with the choices that had actually been made, as represented by the physical structures and appearance of the khipu itself. As I suggested in Chapter 2, this moment of the khipu-kamayuq's querying the construction of the khipu was comparable to that in which an e-mail message, having been transmitted by the sending computer in a series of binary signals, was decoded by the receiving computer into the intended script.

But how were the messages in the khipu actually read? I have suggested possible strategies and procedures for reading or interpreting khipu throughout the course of this study. For example, for the anomalous khipu, reading could have involved the khipukamayuq's learning the conventional translation values for individual knots, as well as for the sets of three knot groups per sets of string arrangements often found on these samples. In addition, we have some evidence that suggests that some khipu were read by translating them into, or interfacing them with, sets or arrays of stones.

Reading Knots with Stones

We are told in the Spanish documents and chronicles that khipukama-yuq would often manipulate stones in reading khipu accounts (Bertonio 1984; Pärssinen 1992; Platt 1987; Urton 1998; see also the references cited in Wassén 1990 [1931]). For example, in one court case concerning the payment in 1579 of tribute to a local *encomendero* (usually a Spaniard who held a grant of patronage over a particular group of Native Americans) by the Indians of the town of Sacaca, in central Bolivia, the local khipukamayuq record keepers read their khipu accounts into the court record. As described by the Spanish scribe at this particular proceeding, the reading was done as follows: "Taking their *quipos* in their hands they said they gave him [the *encomendero*] the following and *placing some stones on the ground by means of which they performed their accounting together with the quipos they said the following* . . ." (cited in Urton 1998: 415; my emphasis; see also Platt 2002). As Tristan Platt and I have both argued, the testimony in this case seems to suggest that the stones were being used by the Sacaca khipukamayuq for making calculations with data recorded on the khipu itself.

Garcilaso de la Vega gave a similar accounting of the procedures for bringing stones into the process of reading tributary khipu:

> At an appointed time the judges responsible for the collection [of tribute] and accountants or scribes who kept the knots and beads for reckoning the tribute assembled in the chief town of the province: the calculations and divisions were made in the presence of the *curaca* [lord] and the Inca governor by means of the knots on the strings and small stones, according to the number of householders in the province. (1966: 274–275)

The above citation from Garcilaso, as well as most others that have been published to date involving the reading of khipu in conjunction with the manipulation of stones (e.g., Murra 1975; Pärssinen 1992: 33–43; Urton 1998), concerns the reading of statistical (esp. tributary) khipu. However, we also find testimony suggesting there was also a tradition of producing more discursive narrative renderings using these two media in combination. For instance, we find one such account in the chronicle written by José de Acosta. After describing the khipu of strings and knots in terms similar to those used by Calancha and Garcilaso, Acosta continues in a passage that I will quote in its entirety:

> In addition to these *quipos* of threads, they have others made of small stones, by means of which they quickly learn the words they want to set to memory, and it is a thing to behold the old, decrepit ones *with a wheel made of small stones* learning the Pater noster, and with another [wheel] the Avemaría, and with another the Credo, and to know which stone signifies: "Who was conceived by the Holy Ghost" and which: "Who suffered under Pontius Pilate." And it is a notable thing to see them correct their mistake when they make an error, for the correction consists in looking at their small stones . . .
>
> There are many of these [wheels of stones] for this purpose in the churchyards; but it is an enchanting thing to see another form of *quipo* in which they use grains of maize, because it is a very intricate accounting, in which a good accountant would be hard put to determine with his pen and ink how much each one should contribute, taking some from over there and adding it over here, and with a hundred other challenges, these Indians will take their grains

and put one here, three over there, eight somewhere else; they move one grain from here, exchanging three from there and, in effect, they finish their accounting promptly without making the slightest error, and they know much better how to do these accounts and give an accounting for what each one ought to pay than we are able to do with pen and ink. Whoever wants may judge whether this is clever or if these people are brutish, but I judge it is certain that, in that which they here apply themselves, they get the better of us. (1954 [1590]: 190; my emphasis)[4]

How could arrays of stones have been manipulated and consulted to read narrative information in khipu? I suggest that khipukamayuq would create arrays of stones, beads, maize kernels, or other "counters"—in a manner similar to the use of the "wheels of stones" described by Acosta—that represented the binary readings of the information encoded in each knot on the khipu in question. In such a (hypothetical) procedure, a given stone would represent one or the other of the possible choices that had been made at each site of binary decision making in the construction of the khipu. In Figure 5.2, I illustrated the linking of the binary choices to pairs of one black stone and one white stone (see Platt 1987: 86–99 and Urton 1997: 191–194 for discussions of the use of black and white stones in Aymara accounting procedures). I am proposing that, in theory, the selection between the differently colored stones would denote which of the two alternative choices for each construction feature had been made in constructing the khipu; this was based on an arbitrary assignment of one stone type to one choice (from a binary pair).

I want to stress that I am proposing the method of binary coding of stones from binary-coded khipu data only for some (unspecified) subset of these knotted-string records. I think that a strong argument for the use of such a procedure by the khipukamayuq can be made, and I will attempt to do so below. However, at this point I cannot give a thoroughly convincing (and certainly not an authoritative) estimate of how commonly such a procedure might have been employed.

In such a procedure, at Level V (Figure 5.2), for example, which is the level of the tying of knots into the string, let us say that a Z-knot will be signed by a white stone, and an S-knot will be signed by a black stone. The result of the process of producing one marker to represent

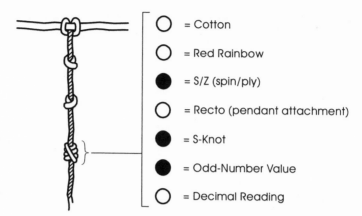

○ = Cotton

○ = Red Rainbow

● = S/Z (spin/ply)

○ = Recto (pendant attachment)

● = S-Knot

● = Odd-Number Value

○ = Decimal Reading

5.4. Binary-coded signature of one knot on a khipu.

the choice that was made at each level of producing a knot would be a sequence of seven stones constituting a display of the totality of the binary-coded information *at any given locus* (i.e., a knot) on a khipu. As I suggested in Chapter 2, this process was similar to the way—in computing information technology—the ASCII code assigns a particular eight-bit sequence of ones and zeros to each stroke on a computer keyboard.

To give an example of the hypothetical mode of constructing a binary-coded sequence of stones as outlined above, take the sequence: ○○●○●●○ (this is the same binary-coded sequence introduced in Chapter 2). The stone array "readout" of this (hypothetical) sequence, using the organization outlined in Figure 5.2 as the key, is shown in Figure 5.4.

Let me reflect briefly on Figure 5.4 from the perspective of a point I made in Chapter 2 about the potential significance of the theory of khipu "reading" that has led us to derive this linear, ASCII-like coding of just one knot on a hypothetical khipu. I noted earlier that even if the theory I am proposing in this book cannot be sustained in future studies, nonetheless, there should be much to be gained for study purposes in the approach proposed here.[5] This is illustrated, for instance, by the seven-bit array displayed in Figure 5.4. This array constitutes a hypothetical "signature" of just one of the 1,536 possible sign units that could have been signed by the khipu binary coding system. Although this signature is distinctive and unique to any knot having all of the relevant qualities, nevertheless, we can suppose that this same signature could be found numerous times in many different khipu samples. In some subset of cases, it may appear repeatedly, either adjacent to, or surrounded by, certain other knots with their distinctive signatures, and in other cases, the neighboring knot signatures may be unlike any found in any other sample.

The point that I am driving at in the above discussion is that, with this new methodology, in which knots are translated into seven-bit coded arrays, we have a tool that can allow us to search through the total corpus of knots on khipu samples in different collections deriving from sites in many different locales. Therefore, this methodology gives us the opportunity, and the controls, to study patterns and variations in khipu construction in ways that have not been possible previously. Perhaps what I have termed knot "signatures" will result, in the end, to have had (for instance) logographic (i.e., glottographic) values—all to the good, then, that we now have a method to search for these distinctive figures in potentially different environments. If it cannot be shown that these signatures had such translation values—that is, as elements of systems of complex mnemonic or writing systems—then we still have this tool available for identifying patterns in the khipu information system.

Coding a Khipu

It is important at this point to provide the reader with a sense of what a total "readout" of the binary coding of a specific khipu would look like. For this example, I am assuming the case in which knots were transcribed into stone arrays. Although (as I have suggested) such transcriptions were performed only for a subset of khipu, I use the example here in order to make visible what a reading might have looked like. I have provided in Table 5.1 the binary coding, according to the black stone/white stone binary choices introduced in Figure 5.2, of one of the khipu (UR19) from the site of Laguna de los Cóndores, in Chachapoyas, northern Peru.[6] For comparative purposes, I have also provided a more standard tabular description of this same khipu in the appendix.

A few explanatory notes are in order regarding the information summarized in Table 5.1. The numbers 1–7 across the top of the table represent the seven (essentially) binary decision-making episodes that must

TABLE 5.1.
Binary Coding of a Khipu (UR19) from Chachapoyas

	Seven-Bit Coded Arrays							
Pendant Number	1	2	3	4	5	6	7	Decimal Value
↓								
1	O	O	O	?	—	—	—	—
2	O	O	O	●	—	—	—	—
3	O	O	O	●	O/O	●/●	O	10/8
3s1	O	✿	O	—	O	O	O	9
4	O	O	O	●	●	O	O	1
5	O	O	O	O	—	—	—	—
6	O	●	O	?	O	O	O	10
6s1	O	O	O	—	—	—	—	—
7	O	O	O	O	O	O	O	1
7s1	O	●	O	—	O	●	O	2
8	O	O	O	●	—	—	—	—
9	O	✿	O	●	O/O/O	●/O/●	O	10/10/8
9s1	O	O	O	—	O	O	O	3
10	O	O	O	●	O/O	●/O	O	10/10
10s1	O	✿	O	—	O	●	O	8
11	O	O	O	●	—	—	—	—
12	O	●	O	●	—	—	—	—
13	O	●	O	O	—	—	—	—
							Total =	100

O = Red/Creator Rainbow or light hue

● = Dark Rainbow or dark hue

✿ = Multicolored

O/O = Two knots on pendant (etc.)

be undergone in order to produce a fully coded information site—a knot—in a khipu. These numbers correspond with what are referred to as "levels" (I–VII) in Figure 5.2. In those cases in which there are multiple knots on a pendant string (i.e., Pendant Nos. 3, 9, and 10), I have placed all the knots on the same line—dividing them by slashes (/)—so as not to have to repeat what is in fact identical information on all counts except (potentially) the knot directionality and odd/even designation of the actual decimal value of the various knots on the string in question. These pieces of information would have to have been (re)coded only once in the display of stone arrays for individual knots.

A few observations and points of clarification should accompany a reading of Table 5.1. In the first place, although knots may carry identical decimal value, those knots may be coded differently for the odd/even (*ch'ulla/ch'ullantin*) classification. For example, in the case of the two single knots on Pendant No. 10, both knots are valued as 10, but the first knot will be classified as odd in its relation to the second even knot. This is in keeping with the principles and rules laid out in Figures 4.3, 4.4, and 4.5, as well as the associated text (see Chapter 4). Similarly, the sole single knot (= 10) on Pendant No. 6 is coded odd according to the principle illustrated in Figure 4.3.

The second thing to note with regard to the data presented in Table 5.1 is that based on the readout signatures created by laying out the arrays of stones (i.e., the series of Os and ●s forming the rows of this table), there appear to be some identical and near identical pieces of information on this khipu. For instance, Pendant Nos. 2, 8, and 11 have the same signature: OOO●. This array may represent a certain "class" of information, and each member of the class may (perhaps) be modified or differentiated from the others by virtue of its particular environment (e.g., the potentially differing signatures of adjacent pendants/arrays).

And finally, with regard to the coding of color in Table 5.1, I will not pretend that I have succeeded in appropriately color-coding this khipu. What I have done is to employ three symbols to signify gross color differences. These three symbols represent a minimal set of contrasts resulting from collapsing and generalizing the two broad categories of binary colors described in Chapter 4. These represent the pairings Red/Creator Rainbow and Dark Rainbow for dyed fabrics, and white/black for the natural hues of cotton and wool. The actual observed and recorded colors in Khipu UR19 are provided in the color column in the tabular description of this same khipu in the appendix. As employed in Table 5.1, the three color/tone symbols have the following values:

O = Red/Creator Rainbow or light wool/cotton color tone
● = Dark Rainbow or dark wool/cotton color tone
✿ = bicolor (i.e., Red/Dark with light/dark)

At this point in our studies of the khipu, what we seek is a source—
an ASCII code–like table—for the translation values for seven-bit sequences like the ○○●○●●○ sequence shown in Figure 5.4 and the
numerous arrays represented in Table 5.1. We now know how to derive thousands, even potentially millions, of such sequences, given that
we can now produce seven-bit coded arrays for every knot tied into
the some 600 surviving khipu in museum collections around the world.
I would stress, however, that to the best of my knowledge there are
at present only 20 samples for which all seven bits of binary-coded
information defined in this study have been recorded; these are the
20 samples from Chachapoyas whose description I only recently
completed.

The Time Dimension in Coding Khipu

We need to pause here to consider an issue relating to the proposed
binary reading technique that becomes evident from a careful look at
Figure 5.4. The question concerns what we might call the seeming cost-
effectiveness of this system of recording and reading. Surely the act of
reading all seven elements of a coded knot would have been quite time
consuming, whether that reading was laid out in stones or not. I estimate that it would have taken one or two seconds to determine the
character of each bit of information in a seven-bit coded khipu knot. In
those cases in which an array of stones was laid out to "transcribe" the
information, I estimate it would have taken some fifteen seconds or so
to produce the complete reading of the different pieces of information
on a knot along any given pendant string (e.g., its material, spin/ply and
attachment patterns, color, knot count and directionality, etc.). I should
also point out that a few bits of information for multiple knots tied
onto the same string would be redundant in certain elements of their
reading. These were the bits that coded for material, spin/ply, and attachment pattern. (For instance, these pieces of information would be
the same for all the knots shown on the pendant string in Figure 5.4.)
Given that a khipukamayuq would only have had to read these three bits
of information once for all knots on this string, he would have had only
four bits of information (i.e., odd/even, knot direction, color [which can
change along the body of a string], and decimal/nondecimal [anoma-
lous] status) to read for each subsequent knot. This would shorten the

time needed to transcribe all of the information on a string from the fifteen seconds *per* knot estimate given above to, perhaps, about ten seconds. Furthermore, it is reasonable to suppose that proficient knot readers would have put to memory the translation values or readings of a large number of knots and (re)coded stone arrays, thus further reducing the time required to move from coded knot, through stone array, to the final reading.

The above estimate of, say, ten to fifteen seconds to read a knot or an array of stones is certainly longer than anything that we alphabet readers (if you are reading this text) are accustomed to. Most of us, I suspect, are capable of reading one-third to one-half a page of not too densely printed text in ten to fifteen seconds or so. Can it have been the case that the Inka (or any other culture) would have relied on a record-keeping system whose time of rendering from code to message was on the order of that estimated above? My answer is that it depends on what kind(s) of "signifying units"—what level of grammatical, semantic denotation—was being signified by the coded units in question. If we were to assume—which I do not necessarily in this study (but see Urton 1998) —that the khipukamayuq recorded, or coded, full sentence-level renderings, including all nouns with full syntactical and semantic markers; verbs with all markers of tense, person, evidentials, etc.; and other grammatical elements, then the system proposed above would have been a rather time-consuming record-keeping method. On the other hand, if the reading of any given knot and stone array produced a mytheme-level unit of information or text, then ten to fifteen seconds is not an excessive amount of time to recover such a relatively large volume of information.

As noted above, elsewhere (Urton 1998) I have argued that the khipukamayuq may well have been recording full subject-object-verb (S-O-V) notations in the khipu. I do not want to completely withdraw from that earlier stated position, or at least not from the theoretical possibility of such record keeping by means of the khipu. In fact, I find it quite suggestive to note that in our analysis of the anomalous Khipu B/8705 in Chapter 4, we found that most pendant strings (87%) on that sample display *three* subunit arrays of knots composing what I termed there the "signifying units" of anomalous khipu. Can such three-unit arrays have been representations of S-O-V constructions? We cannot answer this question with any certainty at the present time.

I want to maintain the theoretical possibility that those subunits could have been, for instance, logosyllabic units arrayed in S-O-V configurations on the pendant strings. However, since we do not yet know what the final solution to our attempts to interpret the khipu will be, we should also keep open a wide range of other possibilities. For example, I see no reason to foreclose the possibility that binary-coded khipu knots could have represented the information for divinatory, oracular, or incantatory renderings. In the latter cases, the fact that it may have taken upward of ten to fifteen seconds to display and decode a sign unit from along a pendant string would not have represented an unacceptable expenditure of time. Rather, in such a charged ceremonial setting, the entire "reading" would have constituted a ritualized event in which the audience would expect to view and experience a full, rich, and lengthy discursive performance based on the decipherment of various strings of a khipu and (possibly) the manipulation of arrays of stones.

These comments all point to the larger and more general problem of just how the Inka may have conceived of and assigned semantic and other possible values to their knotted-string constructions—that is, what was the Inka theory of signs in the khipu? This is the issue we take up in the next chapter.

CHAPTER 6

Sign Theory, Markedness, and Parallelism in the Khipu Information System

I want to address one general reflection on the information presented here on binary coding and two large interpretive issues to bring more focused theoretical and analytical perspectives to the material presented in the preceding chapters. The reflection, which concerns what we could call the "salience" of binary coding, will be taken up immediately below. Of the two larger issues, the first concerns the question: How were signs constituted in this system and how might they have expressed meaning? The second issue concerns the nature of relations between and among the sign units that were twisted, dyed, and tied into the khipu strings. Drawing on comparative and theoretical works dealing with canonical oral and written literatures from various cultures, I will explore how the signs of this recording system may have organized different categories of information and semantic values.

Is Binary Coding Real? And If So, Is It Meaningful?

A couple of concerns may increasingly have come to preoccupy the reader, particularly one who has any familiarity with previous studies of the Inka khipu. These concerns involve the questions: Why is so little of what I have described in this study with respect to binary coding described in previous studies of these devices (for the exception, see Conklin 2002)? And why is virtually nothing about binary construction features mentioned by Spanish chroniclers from the colonial era? I would give two replies to these queries. First and most important, to the best of my knowledge, no one who has studied the khipu up to this time has produced a large body of detailed observations of such khipu construction features as the directionality of spinning, plying, knotting, and string attachment (Conklin describes all of these various features, but he himself does not claim to have documented them with a large number of observations from studies of museum samples). This fact is related to the observation that the overwhelming majority of previous studies of khipu have focused only on the analysis of the patterns of numbers and colors on these devices (e.g., see the sources listed in the bibliography under Marcia and Robert Ascher, Burns, Nordenskiöld, Locke, Radicati di Primeglio, and Zuidema). The point I am driving at here is simply to say that we cannot expect that binary coding would have become a central feature of earlier descriptions and analyses of the khipu if previous researchers did not take note of the features that are constructed in a binary manner.

But why didn't the *chroniclers* mention binary coding if it *was,* indeed, such an important component of this recording system? This question is difficult to answer, especially in regard to chroniclers like the Spaniard Antonio de la Calancha, who made a serious study of these devices; however, it is even more difficult to address when we consider the case of Garcilaso de la Vega, who was the child of an Inka noblewoman (and a conquistador), a native of the old Inka capital, Cusco, and a native speaker of Quechua. As I noted earlier, Garcilaso not only provided extensive and detailed commentary on the khipu in his *Comentarios reales de los incas,* but he also claimed considerable proficiency in reading these devices himself. How could binary coding have been central to khipu coding and decoding when none of the salient features of such a system was even mentioned by Garcilaso?

I confess to having had several sleepless nights trying to answer this last question for myself! I still cannot give a satisfactory answer to this quandary. However, it is precisely this last question that leads me to the second major point I want to make with respect to the significance of binary coding. This is the (unsettling) fact that, even as binary coding has gone unremarked over the centuries since these objects were first encountered by literate Europeans (or by native Andeans who learned to read and write), it (binary coding) *has* unquestionably existed in the very fabric of these devices, and it is there—for anyone who cares to do so—to see, study, and record today. Thus, if one sits for a long time studying samples of khipu closely, noting the directions of spin and ply of every string, knot, and attachment on these devices, one will arrive at the kinds of observations I have reported in this study. The question becomes, then, not whether binary structuring of elements in the khipu

exists, which it undoubtedly does, but rather, whether or not this patterning should be, and was, accorded significance and meaning as a system of coding in the past. Perhaps these varying construction features
were produced randomly or accidentally? Surely they could not have
been produced systematically, with some complicated communication
scheme(s) in mind?

Since the beginning of the colonial era and continuing even to the
present day, there has often been hesitation about according intentionality to the cultural practices of the makers of these complex knotted-
string devices; certainly this was true of many of the (self-assessed) superior, alphabet-using chroniclers of the colonial era. Such was the case,
for instance, when the seventeenth-century Jesuit Bernabé Cobo rendered the following sweeping assessment of native peoples of the Andes:

> [A]ll of them generally coincide in lacking that spirit, that human,
> courteous, and noble manner at which the courtly people of Europe
> excel; for this reason the name *barbarian* is a most apt designation
> for them . . . There is no one who is not surprised and frightened to
> see that these people's power of reason is so dull; this is not so much
> because they are short on reasoning power, as some have alleged, as it
> is because of their very limited mental activity. On the one hand, this
> is because they have no written literature, sciences, or fine arts, which
> generally cultivate, perfect, and make the mind quicker in its opera-
> tions and reasoning powers. Generally they had no natural sciences,
> nor did they usually show craftsmanship in making the things that
> they needed to use for their existence . . . On the other hand, since the
> ingrained, savage vices to which they are commonly given [e.g., he
> mentions intoxication] have nearly become innate, these vices have
> dulled their ingenuity and obscured the light of their powers of rea-
> son. (1983: 21)

Given these sentiments, which characterized the views of many Europeans regarding the descendants of the Inka for much of the early
colonial period, I argue that we lose nothing by setting any such preju-
dices aside and assuming, if for no other reason than that of intellectual curiosity, intelligence and intentionality (as opposed to the opin-
ions expressed by Cobo) on the part of pre-Hispanic and early colonial
Andeans in their production of objects of value, interest, and utility to
themselves—which the khipu surely were.

In this spirit, we return to the question of what we should do with this new knowledge of binary coding. Do we simply discount it and continue, as in the past, only to analyze numbers and colors? In my view, this is not a tenable approach to khipu studies anymore. A long knot of four can no longer simply be that quantitative value alone (though that value can, of course, be interpreted within a quantitative context); rather, any given long knot of four henceforth has become an S- or Z-tied long knot of four on a Z/S- or S/Z-spun/plied dyed cotton or wool string attached to the primary cord in either recto or verso direction. This latter collection of features has become the set of specifications, or distinguishing characteristics, of this particular long knot. Therefore, we must begin to approach the study of khipu with the understanding that all structural and physical features interacted in the semiotic—that is, "sign-using"—processes of the people who looked at and in various other ways consulted these objects. In programmatic terms, it seems clear that the unity of khipu binary structural and other expressive features (e.g., their color and decimal vs. nondecimal environments) intersected and interacted to give rise to the status of individual elements as "signs," and that any given khipu was, as a totality, a "system of signs." The questions become, then: What is a Khipu sign? And what was its system of signs?

A Khipu Sign Theory

As I have proceeded over the past few years to record and analyze khipu construction features, it has become increasingly clear to me that those of us working in this field must begin to develop a general theory of signs that can account for, or motivate, the various structural and linguistic components and patterns of this recording system. The justification for our need for a sign theory is that, given our present lack of understanding of how total messages beyond numerical values (as magnitudes) were encoded and decoded in the khipu, if we do not have a general theory of signs to inform and direct our future research, then (I believe) we can have no sensible idea of how best to advance our studies.

I must also clarify my own position by noting that the fundamental condition or supposition that motivates my sense of our need for a theory of khipu signs is the belief that some, if not all, elements of khipu construction were indeed assigned conventional value by their users. Again, this contrasts with the thinking of those who have adopted what I call the "strong" mnemonic view of the khipu (see Chapter 1), by which I mean the view that these devices were idiosyncratic (i.e., non-conventionalized) constructions onto which information and memories were projected by their individual makers and users by means of private signs and symbols. If such had been the case, then we could not say that khipu were composed of "signs." This is because, as Charles S. Peirce noted in his simple but elegant formulation: ". . . a sign is something by knowing which we know something more" (cited in Johansen 1993: 56). From the perspective of the strong mnemonic interpretation, there would be nothing to know or to be learned from looking at a khipu, because there would be nothing "there" that bore any meaning.

Of course, if in the study of some given script system one has learned how to decipher at least a few sign units, then one does not need a theory of signs—one simply gets on with the business of deciphering the script. This, as I understand it, is more or less the status of work at the present time in the study of the Maya hieroglyphs. Though a limited amount of theorizing goes on at present, particularly with regard to the origins and state of decipherment of the Maya hieroglyphs (see esp. the articles collected in Schmandt-Besserat 1990), for the most part, work in Maya hieroglyphic studies is realized in the hard-going, sign-for-sign, trial-and-error decipherment of well-attested sign units, connecting proposed logographic, syllabic, or logosyllabic values of glyphs to the phonological, syntactic, and semantic properties and values of colonial and contemporary Mayan languages to produce readable texts (see, e.g., Coe 1995; Coe and van Stone 2001; Houston 1996; Schele 1994).

I believe that those of us—the "script-poor" cousins of Mayanists who work in the Andes—pursuing research on the khipu do not have the luxury of being a- or nontheoretical. This is because if we do not develop a productive theory of khipu signs, then, I contend, we have nowhere to go and will continue (as we've done over the past seventy-five years) endlessly massaging the numbers, trying to find meaning in a body of data already well analyzed by experts in numerical analysis. The question becomes, then: Where can we turn in order to develop a theory of khipu signs, recognizing as we now must that the information that is the object of our theorizing consists of: (a) cotton and wool threads of both natural and dyed hues, (b) knots tied into those strings, and (c) a set of construction features that are products of selecting one or the other of two alternative string manipulations, which I have termed here "binary coding"?

In my view, the most fruitful body of work pertaining to sign theory for our purposes is that of Charles Sanders Peirce (1955 [1940]). Peirce understood and theorized signs in terms of relations among three different but interrelated sign types: icon, symbol, and index. It is very difficult to give a brief, straightforward accounting of what Peirce theorized about these three sign types. This is partially because Peirce thought of signs as integrated into an exceedingly complex, multilayered, hierarchical arrangement of types and subtypes that are combined and recombined to produce ten classes of signs (1955: 115–119), but also because, over the course of several decades of a turbulent life in which he worked off and on developing his ideas (see Brent 1993), he produced several different and often contradictory representations of the sign types and classes and of the ways they related to and interacted with each other (see Almeder 1980: 22–33; Johansen 1993: 55–72; and Liszka 1996: 43–52).

Complexity notwithstanding, we should look at some elements of Peirce's sign theory, as there are things to be learned here that can give us a valuable perspective on the *kinds* of signifying objects we may be confronted with in the khipu and the implications this knowledge may have for how to proceed in our study of these objects. In general terms, to have the quality of being a sign means to be capable of determining what Peirce referred to as an interpretant. As James Liszka has noted,

> the interpretant can be understood in its most generous sense as the *translation* of a sign: "a sign is not a sign unless it translates itself into another sign in which it is more fully developed" . . . "meaning [is] in its primary acceptation the translation of a sign into another system of signs" . . . "the meaning of a sign is the sign it has to be translated into . . ." (1996: 24, citing Peirce)

And later:

> If information is expressed propositionally and is the result of a process of inference, still its final import lies elsewhere: ". . . of the myriads of forms into which a proposition may be translated, what is that one which is to be called its very meaning? It is, according to the

pragmatist [e.g., Peirce], that form in which the proposition becomes
applicable to human conduct . . ." It appears that the highest expression of the final interpretant of a sign (or a system of signs), that is,
the translation of a sign, is found in terms of the effects—primarily
in terms of the sorts of habits of conduct established in the interpreting agencies integral to that system of signs. (Liszka 1996: 30, citing
Peirce)

This latter perspective is particularly valuable for our purposes here,
as it emphasizes the original, intimate connection between the objects
(i.e., khipu samples) we view in museums today and the individuals and
communities with which they were related and whose behavior they in-
fluenced in pre-Hispanic and early colonial times (e.g., see the discussion of "communities of practice" in Chapter 2, as well as the fascinating
and highly relevant study by Janet Hoskins [1998] of the link between
objects and narratives in constructions of personal histories in communities in eastern Indonesia).

The three Peircean sign types may be defined from various perspectives; in the following discussion, I characterize the three sign types with
particular reference to the relations of signs to their objects. In these
terms, Peirce defined an *icon* as a sign that resembles its object (e.g., as a
sample or a diagram), an *index* as a sign that stands in a physical relationship to its object (e.g., as smoke [to/for fire], or a weathervane [to/for
the wind]), and a *symbol* as a sign that is assigned a conventional relationship to its object (e.g., as all linguistic signs; Peirce 1955: 104–115;
Skidmore 1981: 45). In Peirce's writings over time, the characterization
of each of these three sign types is further qualified in terms of three
different aspects: presentative, representative, and interpretative. These
may be defined, respectively, as: the sign in regard to its ground; the sign
in regard to its object; and the sign in regard to its interpretant (Liszka
1996: 35). Furthermore (at least as far as we need to follow Peirce's
theory here), each of these latter three subtypes was itself understood in
terms of three different but interrelated qualitative characteristics. For
instance, in the case of the presentative aspect (i.e., the capacity of a sign
to represent its object), Peirce—notorious for neologisms—argued that
sign-type representations could take any one of the trichotomous forms
of the *qualisign* (= tone), the *sinsign* (= token), and the *legisign* (= type;
see Liszka 1996: 34–36).

I wanted to follow a thread of Peirce's typologizing—and trichotom-izing—of sign types in order to be able to introduce the *sinsign,* for it seems to me that this sign form may prove especially useful to us in de-veloping a general grounding for a theory of khipu signs. The question confronting us obviously becomes: What *is* a "sinsign," and what could this sub-subtype of Peircean sign forms have to do with the types of con-structions we are concerned with here—that is, the collections of binary construction tasks that were performed in the production of khipu sign units? David Savan has given a characterization of the sinsign (token) that clarifies the relevance of this sign type for thinking about khipu con-struction features and for the ways in which they may be said to denote meaning—that is, the ways the various features of khipu may relate not only to their intended referents but also to the intellectual and recording traditions whose characteristics they are the physical manifestation of:

> The samples of moon rock being analyzed by lunar scientists are *sin-signs.* Every singularity and peculiarity of the moon rock is recorded, analysed, and used as a clue or sign of the structure and history of the moon, the earth, and the solar system. *Whenever some object or event is used as a clue to some other object or event past, present, or spatially at some remove, this clue is a sinsign.* A clue like the moon rock is in fact *a collection of clues.* Every peculiarity of the rock, every molecule of it, is significant as a possible clue to the past. (cited in Johansen 1993: 68–69; my emphases)

By analogy with the example given above, I suggest that an apt char-acterization of what we are dealing with in our studies of the khipu today is that these devices constitute collections of clues (sinsigns) ". . . to some other object or event past, present, or spatially at some remove." I argue that the proper objective of our examination of these clues/sinsigns ought not (at least not at this stage) be the actual mes-sages encoded on any particular khipu; rather, we should view the khipu binary-coded features as informative of the total, conventionalized in-formation system standing behind and informing the production and use of khipu. That is, I suggest that study of khipu sinsigns—tokens, or "clues to the past"—may help us begin to understand the frame-work of conventional values and patterned construction elements, and their standard combinations and recombinations, that the khipukamayuq shared, worked with, and reproduced in encoding and decoding messages in the khipu.

In sum, the perspective on khipu signs that I suggest we adopt is to see them as tokens, or sinsigns, of the intellectual, syntactic, semantic, and other elements of the system of information of the communities of practice that produced and manipulated khipu as a whole. As a part of this strategy, I propose to introduce a new perspective from which to evaluate and value the sets of khipu signs and clues that we now understand to have been of a *binary* nature. This perspective, which I outline and undertake to develop in some detail below, is "markedness theory."

Structure and Hierarchy in the Khipu Signs

Perhaps the best place to begin defining markedness is with its earliest articulation in an exchange of letters, dating from 1930, between two Russian linguists, Nikolaj Trubetzkoy and Roman Jakobson. Jakobson would go on to develop markedness theory in its most elaborate and extensive forms over the course of the next forty years (Eco 1977; Holenstein 1974). As Trubetzkoy wrote concerning paired, or correlative, phonemic elements in certain linguistic constructions:

> Statistics has nothing to do with it. And the essence lies in the so-to-speak "intrinsic content" of the correlation. Apparently any . . . phonological correlation acquires in the linguistic consciousness the form of *a contraposition of the presence of a certain mark to its absence* (or of the maximum of a certain mark to its minimum). Thus, one of the terms of the correlation necessarily proves to be "positive," "active," and the other becomes "negative," "passive." (cited in Waugh 1982: 300; my emphasis)

In his reply, Jakobson noted (among other things):

> I am coming increasingly to the conviction that your thought about correlation as a constant mutual connection between a marked and unmarked type is one of your most remarkable and fruitful ideas. It seems to me that it has a significance not only for linguistics but also for ethnology and the history of culture, and that such historico-cultural correlations as life~death, liberty~non-liberty, sin~virtue, holidays~working days, etc., are always confined to relations *a*~

non-a, and that it is important to find out for any epoch, group, nation, etc., what the marked element is. (cited in Waugh 1982: 300; my emphasis)

In essence, the notion of markedness focuses on the relations between linked pairs or dyadic sets of phonological or grammatical elements, or word meanings, that are in a relationship of asymmetrical (hierarchical) binary opposition to each other. One of the items (the marked member of the set) will be more narrowly specified with respect to some feature than the other (the unmarked member), the latter of which is the more general term. The unmarked term, then, is *less* narrowly specified than the marked term. Another way to express such relationships is in terms of the unmarked category or term acting to establish the general "ground" of the binary pair in question, while the marked term denotes a narrower, more highly specified domain within the general grounding established by the unmarked term. As regards the hierarchical relations between the two parts of such paired elements, the unmarked term is usually hierarchically superior to the marked term (for a broad range of studies on markedness, see Andrews 1990; Battistella 1996; Fox 1974, 1977; Holenstein 1974: 121–132; Mannheim 1998; Pomorska and Rudy 1985; van Schooneveld 1977; and Waugh 1982, 1985).

An aspect of markedness that is the topic of considerable theorizing concerns the way(s) in which the marked and unmarked categories relate to—especially differ from—each other. In general, these relations take either of two forms: (a) *A/non-A:* a type of binary opposition—often referred to as a relation of specified absence (i.e., the nonsignalization of A), exclusion, or neutralization—involving the opposition of paired terms by way of the specification of some value in the marked category (A) and its absence in the unmarked category (non-A; for example, voiced/nonvoiced, colorful/noncolorful, etc.); and (b) *A/B:* a type of binary opposition taking the form of polar opposites (i.e., the signalization of non-A [= signalization of B]), in which A and B are opposed terms within a unified evaluative domain (e.g., vocalic/consonantal, day/night, life/death; see Andrews 1990: 9–19; Battistella 1996: 7–18; Jakobson 1985; and Utaker 1974: 80–81).

I will discuss the matter more fully in a moment, but what has been said thus far about markedness should prompt us to wonder whether or not the universe of binary oppositions in the khipu that we have described in such detail in earlier chapters may represent a highly structured system for organizing relations between marked and unmarked sign values. We may ask, in turn, if this organizational framework informed the narrative constructions that were "read" from/in these devices. I will clarify a few more issues regarding markedness theory in general before turning directly to consider the relevance of these ideas for interpreting the signs and sign system of the khipu and of the ways they may constitute clues to the information system of these devices (e.g., its markedness and other values).

Linguists investigating the forms and variations of markedness relations over the years have suggested a number of evaluative criteria for the patterns of hierarchical relations between marked and unmarked categories. Here, we should mention in particular Joseph Greenberg's (controversial) notion that *frequency* may be one of the most useful diagnostics of markedness; that is, Greenberg argued that the *unmarked* term of some given binary opposition should be the one that occurs most frequently (Greenberg 1966, 1977; Holenstein 1974: 133–134; for reservations about the significance of frequency in markedness theory, see Battistella 1996: 14, 50–51). A related notion is the suggestion, by Edith Moravicsik and Jessica Wirth, that in a binary opposition, ". . . the one of the two entities that is consistently more widely distributed and/or simpler and/or more richly elaborated is called 'unmarked'" (cited in Battistella 1996: 14). As Edwin Battistella points out, this passage reflects the tension that exists in much of the literature on the diagnostics of markedness, in which, on the one hand, asymmetry is sometimes seen as fundamental (e.g., Greenberg's views on "frequency") or, on the other hand, the pairs of terms are simply seen as correlative (e.g., as in the second part of the citation from Moravicsik and Wirth, above; we will return to this issue below).

The above suggestions may bring to the reader's mind the data pertaining to knot directionality discussed in Chapter 3 (esp. Table 3.3). We saw there, for instance, that Z-knots are more commonly and widely distributed than S-knots. Are we therefore justified in arguing that, in some setting in which knot directionality might have been used at least partially to sign paired values in binary opposition to each other (e.g., male/female, local/foreign, alive/dead), the unmarked categories (i.e., the first of each pair listed here) may have been signed by Z-knots? To make such a case, we might want (among other things) to be confident in our interpretation of handedness in Inka/Quechua symbolism. That is, when I (a right-hander) tie a single, or overhand, knot, it takes the form of a Z-knot. Linda Waugh has noted that handedness is a domain of markedness and that right-handedness is virtually everywhere more common and hierarchically superior (i.e., *un*marked) vis-à-vis left-handedness (Waugh 1982: 314; see the classic study on the symbolism of handedness in Hertz 1973 [1909]). As I noted earlier (Chapter 2), right-handedness is not only predominant in work in Andean communities today, but it was also more highly valued, as portrayed in the descriptions of Inka symbolism and ritual practices in the Spanish chronicles. For instance, as Juan de Matienzo detailed this point in the mid-sixteenth century:

> In each *repartimiento* or province there are two divisions: one is called *hanansaya,* and the other *hurinsaya.* . . . [T]he curaca of the hanansaya division is the principal lord of all the province; the other curaca of hurinsaya obeys him when he speaks. He of the hanansaya has the best position of the seats and in all the other places they repeat this order. Those of the hanansaya division seat themselves at the right-hand side, and those from the hurinsaya at the left-hand side. . . . This leader from hanansaya is the principal of all and he has domination over those of hurinsaya. (1967 [1567, Pt. 1, Chap. 6]: 20)

The principal difficulty with the formulation given above, in which handedness is attributed a particular markedness value, is that markedness is generally considered to be context specific and thus potentially changeable. For instance, given two terms—A/B—in which, in a given context, A is considered hierarchically superior to B, a change in context can result in a reversal in the hierarchical positions of the pair of terms. Waugh gives the example (from American culture) involving the binary opposition female/male in which female is marked (i.e., "special") in the context of the professoriate or for medical doctors, whereas male is marked for the job occupations of secretary and nurse (Waugh 1982: 310). This considerably complicates any neat, formulaic attributions of markedness and makes it clear that what is required in each such instance is a deep understanding of the cultural contexts of the meanings and markedness of terms in the language(s) and culture(s) under investigation.

Social Dualism and Binary Oppositions

In order to determine whether or not markedness theory may be a useful approach in analyzing khipu signs, we begin by reminding ourselves of the particular features of the sign system that set us on this search for a theoretical grounding for khipu binary coding. What we could call the paradigmatic operation by means of which khipu are constructed, bit by bit, from raw materials—wool or cotton and dyes—is constituted in a series of tasks that the khipu maker performed that involved selecting one or the other of two alternative construction operations. I argue that these operations reflect (and reproduce) two different types of binary oppositions. One type was based on the *physical manipulations* of objects (e.g., strings) in one *or* the other of two mutually exclusive ways. For example, the khipu maker could spin a thread at one moment *either* counterclockwise *or* clockwise. Similarly, he/she could attach a pendant string by moving the closed end of the string *either* under *or* over and then around the primary cord. However, we should bear in mind that although only one or the other of these two types of operations could be performed in any one construction event (based as they are on mutual exclusivity), nonetheless, as a system of *binary* coding, the total corpus of khipu displays examples of *both* types of operations.

The second type of operation involved in khipu construction is one in which the alternative productions were in a relationship of *symbolic opposition*, rather than having been physically mutually exclusive. This second type pertains to the operations that resulted especially in the binarisms of khipu number values (decimal vs. nondecimal) and colors (Puka/Kamaq K'uychi vs. Lutu K'uychi). Unlike the operations involved in the manufacture (e.g., spin/ply) of strings and in their attachment to the primary cord, the khipu maker could execute the two different types of number and color binarisms on the same string—even on the same knot. For instance, there could be two completely different classes of colors on the same string (i.e., with either one being replaced by the other down the length of the string, or with the two being spun together, barber-pole fashion); these different classes may be dark and light natural-hued fibers or threads dyed in Puka/Kamaq and Lutu rainbow hues. Similarly (as we have seen in Chapter 4), decimal and nondecimal numerical values can be combined on the same string (e.g., a single knot in the tens position coupled with a long knot of 11, which together give a quantity of 21 or some narrative [nonquantitative] value). Thus, on the one hand, we are confronted in the khipu with a total system based on the principle of *dualism,* while, on the other hand, this dualism exists within the context of *binary oppositions* (i.e., each sign element being one or the other of two possibilities).

I argue that we need to take into account the two different types of binary oppositions—mutual exclusion and symbolic opposition—as we develop a khipu sign theory, because the two types of operations and oppositions may have encoded different types or classes of information. This would be consistent with theories of binary opposition and markedness in linguistics, in which, as we have seen, it is recognized that binary oppositions may be composed in the forms (a) A/non-A (= exclusivity; e.g., voiced/nonvoiced) and (b) A/B (= polarity; e.g., vocalic/consonantal; see Utaker 1974). In these terms, it is interesting to think about what the possible significance might have been in the khipu of the use of, for example, an S-knot rather than a Z-knot. That is, was S read as *non*-Z? Or was S read as S, Z read as Z, with there being no necessary (logical) connection between any two such meanings? More specifically, was S (or Puka/Kamaq K'uychi) a given quality or value, and Z (or Lutu K'uychi) its *absence*? Or did S and Z (or Puka/Kamaq K'uychi and Lutu K'uychi) represent quite different, even potentially unrelated, qualities?

An important issue concerning how such binary elements as those discussed above may have been read in relation to one another is the matter of the presence of asymmetric, hierarchical relations between terms or elements in a state of binary opposition to each other. This is a way of asking more pointedly, assuming that such relations *were* asymmetrical: How might markedness relations have entered into khipu signing practices? And where might we see models or expressions of such relations elsewhere in the society under investigation?

Although the following is a controversial claim (as I will show below), I argue that we can look for relevant models and comparisons for strategies of embedding hierarchical binary oppositions in khipu sign structures in the symbolic values reflected in Andean dualistic socio-cultural systems. For instance, in many Andean communities past and present, social and political identity and action were realized in people's belonging to one or the other of two moiety groupings. The moieties were, and in some cases still are, referred to by such designations as *hanan* (upper) and *hurin* (lower; Urton 1990; Zuidema 1964), or *qollana* (upper/right) and *sawqa* (lower/left; Palomino Flores 1970: 79–82). In every such case that I am aware of, the two halves of a symbolic social whole are in an asymmetrical relationship to each other for some specified value or measure (e.g., upper/lower; right/left; senior/junior; older/younger). Asymmetry in such settings is usually expressed as one member of the opposing pair being considered to encompass, be superior to, or have priority or precedence over the other (as we saw in the quote from Matienzo earlier; see also the highly relevant study of dualism and hierarchical relations in Inka sociopolitical organization in Gose 1996).

I would emphasize the point that the type of social systems described above are systems of *dual* organization in which a community is organized so that the two parts (moieties) are in *opposition* to each other, and their *unity* constitutes the social whole. However, although it is essential to have both moieties for a complete, functioning social organization to exist, at the individual level, each person generally can belong only to one *or* the other of the two groups. Recognizing that there are exceptions to every rule and that one should never say "never," individuals in communities in the Andes organized into moieties usually belong only to one or the other of the moieties, "never" to both.[1]

Now, the point I am driving at above is to suggest that Andean moiety systems, or dual and binary social organizations, may provide models for opposition, complementarity, and *weighting* (i.e., asymmetry) as they may have operated in the binary coding of the khipu sign system, particularly to the extent that the information encoded in the sign system was consulted to (re)construct histories and other types of narrations representing community social, political, and ritual relations. That is, for each of the (seven) operations undertaken in the construction of khipu signs, the total universe of surviving intact khipu display a *dual* organization. For instance, some knots are S-knots, while others are Z-knots; thus, globally, khipu are composed of *both* S- *and* Z-knots (i.e., just as a given community is made up of both "upper" *and* "lower" people). However, at the level of each individual feature, this is a system of binary opposition; for example, any given knot is *either* S *or* Z, just as in our exemplary community, each individual is *either* "upper" *or* "lower." In sum, the khipu signing system, as is true with many Andean community organizations past and present, is based equally on dualism and hierarchical binary opposition.

Beyond the forms of structural (i.e., construction) analogs between binary-coded khipu and Andean dual organizations, we can add a couple of more direct comparisons. For example, we may be reminded of the information discussed earlier (Chapter 2) from Frank Salomon's study of the paired khipu and *ayllu* of Tupicocha. In this community, Salomon found that a pair of khipu—distinguished from each other in at least one dimension by spin/ply directionality—were the patrimony of a pair of *ayllu*, one junior, the other senior. Now, it is often the case that, in the opposition between young and old, these are often valued, respectively, as marked and unmarked (e.g., Battistella 1996: 16; Waugh 1982: 309). If this is the character of the hierarchical relation between these categories in Tupicocha, which would have to be determined on empirical grounds, this would result in an asymmetrical (marked/unmarked, junior/senior) pair of *ayllu* linked to a pair of khipu. On the surface at least, this would appear to be an embodiment of the kind of connection I have theorized above concerning the relation between social dualism and khipu binary organization.[2]

The other piece of evidence I would add to this mix is drawn from my own recent analysis of one of the khipu from the site of Laguna de los Cóndores, in Chachapoyas, northern Peru (Urton 2001). In studying one very large khipu sample from this site, I found that this khipu appears to have been organized into a two-year calendar by the organization of discrete sets of pendant strings. Specifically, there are 24 groups of pendants averaging 29–31 pendant strings per group, for a total of 730 pendant strings in the calendar. I argue in the study cited above that this khipu registered a pair of years (i.e., $2 \times 365 = 730$ strings/days) and that this two-year khipu calendar contains an accounting of the labor tribute owed—or possibly completed—by the 3,000 local tribute payers to Inka state projects in the region. There is a significant asymmetry in the number of tribute payers registered on the khipu from one year (ca., 1,000) to the next (ca. 2,000). Here, again, we could argue that this pair of years registered on a tributary khipu calendar reflects the link between social dualism and asymmetrical (i.e., weighted or hierarchical) binary oppositions in record keeping that I have suggested in this section was so important in Inka administration and accounting practices.

The central question that we come to now is: Were hierarchy and asymmetrical relations also elements of the khipu binary-coding sign system? That is, were the dual/binary elements of khipu coding—like those of the dual/binary elements of Andean social organization, in which both were necessary but one was privileged over, or hierarchically superior to, the other—also hierarchically related to each other? I hypothesize that the answer to this question is yes—for example, by the principle of "insistence" and for other reasons to be argued below. If this supposition is correct, then markedness theory may provide a useful analytical tool for us to apply as we begin constructing and querying a framework of relations, values, and potentially even meanings in the khipu sign system.

Before turning to examples of markedness in khipu binary constructions, we must recognize that to claim a connection between binary opposition in linguistic, semantic coding and dualism in social organization is quite controversial and disputed by some authors. Bruce Mannheim, for instance, argues that the two domains are distinct and should not be confused or mixed up with one another (1998: 264–265; see also Fox 1977: 81). In general terms, I would also urge caution in arguing for the convergence of sociopolitical dualism and binary symbolic values, particularly if what is suggested is some kind of universal proposition supposing that dualism governed all human action (e.g., as has been claimed for the appeal of binary categories in "normal" structural analysis). The issue that we face in the khipu, however, is a more limited, narrowly motivated (i.e., directed) kind of connection. What is at issue here is not whether all human cultural action is, at base, dualistic, but whether when record keepers who lived in Andean communities that were organized into hierarchical moiety organizations went about constructing statistical accounts and historical representations of those dualistic communities, they would have done so in terms of grammatical and semantic formulations and signing systems that were built on asymmetric, binary terms and relations—as were the processes of social reproduction of the social systems themselves. Thus, we are concerned here with reportative functions and processes, not normative, universalist claims. As such, I argue that hypothesizing connections between marked/unmarked binary khipu signs in narrating histories of communities organized according to asymmetrical, hierarchical structures constitutes a legitimate form of comparison and argumentation.

Signs of Markedness in the Khipu

We turn finally to consider how markedness might have played a role in organizing and valuing information registered by means of binary coding in the Inka khipu. The suggestions listed below are premised on two fundamental propositions about the nature of this record-keeping system: First, this was a system of "signs"; thus (in Peirce's terms), there was something to be learned by viewing the patterns of binary constructions encoded in these devices. And second, as James Fox has argued, in any semantic theory—which, I maintain, is what we are developing here—". . . opposition without hierarchy can only lead to endless manipulations" (1975: 118); therefore, I think that the binary values of the khipu signs were hierarchically related to each other. Since markedness applies to paired (dyadic) sign units that are hierarchically related to each other, I argue that markedness may have been a critical feature of the khipu sign system. The question is, where do we see such relations? I list below several possible areas in which the exclusivity and differential frequency and distribution of construction elements may be interpreted as differences in weighting (i.e., markedness) that underlay the semantic values of the information recorded in these devices.

(a) In the realm of color, we have the binary categories Puka/Kamaq K'uychi and Lutu K'uychi. As the more narrowly specified color class (i.e., Red/*Creator* Rainbow), Puka/Kamaq K'uychi would clearly constitute the marked category, as opposed to Lutu K'uychi (Dark Rainbow), the unmarked category.

(b) If we accept the proposition put forward by Greenberg and others that frequency is an important measure of markedness, with the element(s) occurring most frequently representing the *un*marked category of some binary, perhaps antonymic, pair, then, for instance, the table showing the frequency and distribution of different knot directionality patterns (Table 3.3) could be read as a table of markedness. As we see in Table 3.3, the knot pattern displaying Z-type single, long, and figure-eight knots is roughly twice as common as the pattern displaying S-knots in all three positions. Thus, in the surviving khipu samples, Z-knots might have been used to signify unmarked semantic categories, social statuses, symbolic values, or other properties in opposition to their more narrowly specified (marked) counterparts, the latter of which would have been signed by means of S-knots. A relevant datum here (though producing different directional/markedness values), again, is Salomon's material from Tupicocha in which a khipu with predominantly Z-spun/S-plied threads belongs to a senior *ayllu* of a pair, the junior *ayllu* of which curates a khipu with predominantly S-spun/Z-plied threads (Salomon 2002: 305).

(c) Looking at the binary-coded khipu (UR19) in Table 5.1, we see under columns 1 (= material), 3 (= spin/ply), and 7 (= decimal reading) that all these features in this sample are coded in the same way (= O). Thus, *for Khipu UR19* (i.e., this is not necessarily a generalizable statement), these elements should relate to unmarked semantic values.

(d) In Table 4.1, which displays the transcription of values of a section of pendant strings on the "anomalous" Khipu B/8705, we should note the relative frequency, for instance, of nondecimally arrayed single-knot values as opposed to long-knot values, as well as of odd (*ch'ulla*) numerical values as opposed to even (*ch'ullantin*) ones. These frequency measures could suggest a distribution of markedness over the "signifying units" of this anomalous, nondecimal khipu sample.

(e) As for the odd/even (*ch'ulla/ch'ullantin*) values themselves, I suggest that this constitutes a binary opposition of the mutually exclusive "neutralization" type (i.e., A/non-A), rather than one of the polarity type (A/B). This would be the case in situations where there is no notable frequency differential with respect to the registration of these (complementary) values; in such cases, I imagine the unmarked category is *ch'ulla* (the odd one), and the marked (i.e., more highly specified) category would be *ch'ullantin* (the one linked intimately to the odd one); however, if there is a notable difference in the frequency of representation of one or the other of these numerical values (e.g., see item [d], above), then the most commonly displayed category would represent (i.e., sign) the unmarked semantic value.

Binary Coding in the Khipu as a Form of Parallelism

By the end of the above discussion of markedness, I believe it is not rash to claim that this new perspective on the khipu provides us with a methodological and theoretical grounding to begin to identify something resembling an organization of (and for) grammatical structures in the binary code of the Inka khipu. This, I argue, moves us a little farther along the road to a decipherment of these records, if they are indeed decipherable. Alternatively, if these records do not in the end prove to be susceptible to decipherment, then the new perspective I have introduced above may convince us of their indecipherability more readily than might otherwise have been the case. As should be clear by this point, I maintain considerable optimism on the question of the ultimate decipherability of these ancient knotted-string records.

But we should now ask: Have we carried our analysis and theorizing of khipu signs as far as we are able to at the present time? I think we can, in fact, go one step further and that, in doing so, we will be able to sketch out a structuring of meanings in these devices that will take us much nearer to developing an approach that may prove fruitful in attempting to decipher the khipu. The concept that I want to introduce and explore—though we are able to do so now only rather sketchily—is referred to as *parallelism*. This was another of the central topics of interest and concern for the great structural linguist Roman Jakobson (1966, 1985; see also Fox 1988; Mannheim 1998; Tedlock 1983; and Waugh 1985: 150–151). The original formulation of the principle of parallelism as a general poetic form was in the work of the eighteenth-century Oxford scholar Robert Lowth, a noted authority in the field of Hebrew poetry. As Lowth phrased the matter:

> The correspondence of one verse or line with another, I call parallelism. When a proposition is delivered, and a second is subjoined to it, or drawn under it, equivalent, or contrasted with it in sense, or similar to it in the form of grammatical construction, these I call parallel lines; and the words or phrases, answering one to another in corresponding lines, parallel terms. (cited in Fox 1988: 5)

Jakobson was particularly interested in what he referred to as "canonical parallelism." This was a type of parallel construction in which the coupling of phonological, morphological, or semantic figures took on obligatory forms and figures in the ritualized recitation of oral poetry in various cultural traditions. Fox (1988) has documented the presence of canonical parallelism in diverse discursive traditions of Europe, Asia, and the Americas. For instance, Fox cites the example of canonical parallelism as incorporated in curing chants among the Chamula, a Tzotzil Mayan–speaking group in southern Mexico (see Gossen 1974: 211–212). A portion of one such chant is rendered:

> I seek you in this petition
> I seek you in this cure, my lord
> For the payment lies at your feet
> For the payment lies before your hands . . .
>
> (cited in Fox 1977: 75)

In these lines, the parallel terms are "petition/cure," and "feet/hands." Certain regular features typify the construction of parallelisms in (oral) literatures around the world. For example, terms usually change in the initial or final position of verses (though they may change in the middle), and, as is evident in many of the comparative examples discussed by Fox, given that often only one word changes in adjacent verse lines, there is a tremendous redundancy—thus a high "memorability"—in such forms of versification (Fox 1977: 75). Before moving to address directly the issue of parallelism in Quechua poetics, I should note that, in his own studies of canonical parallelism among the Rotinese in Timor, Indonesia, Fox found that virtually all elements in these poetic constructions had to be paired; that is, each element formed a part of what he refers to as "dyadic sets" (1974, 1988). Specialists in the ritual language in Roti are required to know up to 1,000–1,500 of these linked pairs (cf. the number of khipu binary signs, which was 1,536; see Chapter 5), or dyadic sets, in order to be considered to have achieved minimal fluency (Fox 1974: 79). As for the production of these sets in recitation:

[I]t is only as one grows old that true mastery of the language is possible. Without a detailed knowledge—the knowledge of the necessary and unique pairing of specific species of named trees, fish, insects, of particular cultural objects, or, for example, of certain emotionally expressive verbs—without this, an individual poet does not

have this true mastery . . . Since any mistake in these pairs is immediately detectable and—among Rotinese—quickly challenged, an
aspiring poet must have a firm command of a good number of these
unique pairs before he begins to compose. (Fox 1977: 79)

The astute reader may have already deduced where I am taking this
comparison to such canonical parallelistic traditions as that of the Rotinese, briefly characterized above. That is, I argue that the world of poetic,
narrative production grounded in "dyadic, or paired, sets" is a world
with which our khipukamayuq, working daily with their records produced in "binary code," would have been quite familiar. In fact, we can
draw a poignant comparison between the labors of the Rotinese ritual
poet, characterized in the quotation above from Fox's research, and the
description given by Calancha of the hard labors of the khipukamayuq
who had to study their knotted records intensely:

> . . . and the Quipo Camayos, whether because of the privileges with
> which they honored the office, or because if they did not give good
> accounting about that on which they were questioned they were
> severely castigated, were continually studying the signs, ciphers, and
> relations [of the khipu], teaching them to those who would succeed
> them in office . . . The Secretary, or Quipo Camayo, was at the pain
> of death . . . if he lost some of the truth, or ignored something
> that he should know about, or if he diverged from accounts of the
> deeds, legacies, or oracles it [the khipu] contained. (1974: 205; my
> translation)

The critical question is: What can we say, or theorize, about the contents of the records that the khipukamayuq pored over, as described by
Calancha? I argue that he studied "canonical parallelisms"—which, as
we will see, are referred to in the Andean literature as "semantic couplets"—embedded in the khipu. These would have been registered by
way of the binary sign system. In this system, I submit, any given registered value would have been the member of the "dyadic set"—i.e., one
element of the canonical binary pair—that was called for in the narrative in question. We have not previously encountered suggestions that
markedness (as it involves the weighting of binary pairs) is related to
the paired sets of parallelism. However, such a linkage was recognized
by Jakobson (1966: 399), and Fox has noted as well from his research

in Roti that ". . . parallelism is an extension of the binary principle of opposition to the phonetic, syntactic, and semantic levels of expression. Poetic language is the most elaborate and complex expression of this phenomenon" (1988: 3).

To turn now to the potential application of markedness and parallelism to the analysis of the khipu, the central body of work for us to take into account concerning Quechua is that by the linguist Bruce Mannheim (1986, 1998). In his studies of what he refers to as "semantic couplets," Mannheim is more explicit than many other linguists in emphasizing a connection between markedness and parallelism. Specifically, Mannheim argues that the sequential ordering of the paired elements composing semantic couplets corresponds to hierarchies of meaning, with the more general, unmarked member preceding the more highly specified, marked member. As he states the matter, ". . . the relative hierarchy of each pair is projected onto the sequence of the terms in couplets, so that the couplet becomes a *diagrammatic icon* of the conceptual relationship" (1998: 257; my emphasis). Mannheim has explored the incorporation of these principles in particular in the organization of semantic pairs in contemporary Andean *waynus*, which are the current, traditional "folk/country" songs of the western South American highland regions (Mannheim 1998: 258–263).

Most important for my attempt here to link the poetic strategy of semantic couplets with the binary structuring of the khipu sign system is that this form of poetry is encountered in the colonial Quechua literature as well. For example, we find the following segment of ritual poetry in the early-seventeenth-century chronicle written by the native southern Peruvian chronicler Juan de Santa Cruz Pachacuti Yamqui:

Intiqa	Sun
Killaqa	Moon
P'unchawqa	Day
Tutaqa	Night
Puquyqa	the season of ripeness
Chirawqa	the season of freshness
Manam yanqachu	do not simply exist
Kamachisqam purin	[but] are ordered

(cited in Mannheim 1998: 245)

The semantic couplets in the above poem are composed of linked verses occupying adjacent lines, with the unmarked terms in lines 1, 3, 5, and 7 and their (respective) paired, marked terms in lines 2, 4, 6, and 8. The numerical notation used here makes explicit and compelling a possible connection between these semantic couplets and binary elements of the khipu coding system discussed earlier—that is, the relationship between odd (*ch'ulla*) and even (*ch'ullantin*) number values (see Chapter 4).

In concluding his exposition, Mannheim argues that the poetry of Quechua semantic couplets

> . . . provides a partial map of the conceptual organization of the Quechua lexicon. . . . The structural alignment between the members of a pair focuses the semantic properties that are associated with each word stem and enhances their cognitive retention. . . . Semantic couplets, then, are both a means by which lexical relations are transmitted and reproduced among Quechua speakers . . . and a heuristic by means of which the ethnographer can explore culture through discourse . . . (1998: 267–268)

My purpose in spending a considerable amount of time on Mannheim's treatment of semantic couplets is to advance the hypothesis that this material provides us with a paradigmatic approach to canonical parallelism—incorporating markedness values and relations—as an explanation for the overall architecture of binary-coded elements in at least the narrative ("anomalous") Inka khipu. I confess that I do not know now exactly how to flesh out this hypothesis in terms of the particular forms and patterning of binary structures that we encounter in the extant khipu. That is, how should we suppose the semantic couplets were represented (as I am arguing here they were) in the binary-coded elements of the khipu?

Two possible answers to the question raised above seem to present themselves most obviously. One possibility is that any given binary-coded element in a khipu represents a sign for a *canonical pair*. For example, and to return for a moment to the binary-coded khipu knot ○○●○●●○ that was introduced in Chapter 2 and further explicated in Chapter 5 and Figure 5.4, we could say that this represents the "signature" of a canonical, lexical pair—a dyadic set that was considered to be (onto)logically connected in some fundamental way, such as in the semantic couplet: *inti* (sun)/*killa* (moon). In this view, the knot, as well as its (potential) binary (re)coding in stones, would have constituted a conventionalized representation (i.e., a sign in the form of a "diagrammatic icon") of a particular canonical pair and would, therefore, have prompted its recitation by the khipukamayuq. The other possibility that presents itself immediately is that any given binary-coded knot was "read" by the khipukamayuq in relation to some other (adjacent? opposed?) knot; the two would have been conceived of and read as linked, canonical pairs. An example would be the suggestion made above for linking the odd (unmarked) and even (marked) lines of poetry with these respective numerical coding values in the khipu binary coding system. I do not have any grounds, or logic, from which to privilege one of these interpretations over the other.

As for the content of the binary figures, or semantic couplets, signed (possibly) by one or the other of the means outlined above, I suggest (in addition to the kinds of poetic constructions noted above) that we consider various *classes of meanings* that might have been of interest to the Inka state officials—the khipukamayuq—who made and consulted these devices. For example, one such class of meanings may have referred to interrelated, hierarchically opposed *qualities* in the systems of classification central to the social, political, and economic organizations of the Inka Empire. These might have included such oppositions—expressible as unmarked/marked classes of objects, or semantic couplets—as *hanan/hurin*, Inka/non-Inka, male/female, senior/junior, my group/not my group, domesticated/wild, or past/present (see also Billie Jean Isbell's [1985] discussion of markedness relations in Andean human-animal metaphors).

A second class of meanings could have signed paired but opposed *operations*. These might have been used to denote such complementary or reciprocal actions as addition/subtraction, multiplication/division, and collection/(re)distribution. Such formulations could have been employed, for example, in moving through a historical narration or in giving an account of the formation and dissolution of kin groups (e.g., moieties, or *ayllu*) over time.

It is easy to talk in general terms about possible classes of linked and/or opposed hierarchically related meanings with markedness values, such as those mentioned above, and quite another thing to imagine how we might go about identifying and assigning such meanings to specific elements of a khipu and then testing or verifying the relevance and validity of those interpretations for the khipu in question. However, as I have suggested elsewhere (Urton 1998), I believe that the most reasonable way to approach such a task would be to begin with a careful study of the transcriptions of khipu contained in colonial Spanish documents. As John Murra (1975) has shown convincingly, such documents often provide information concerning the "ethnocategories" of objects by means of which the early colonial descendants of the Inka organized information in the khipu. I have suggested that we may expand the types of information signed by the khipu to include ethnocategories of actions in state labor service (Urton 1998, 2001). Such ethnocategories of objects and actions as may be derived from native readings of khipu in colonial times could serve as points of departure for developing inventories of classes of meanings recorded in semantic couplet-like arrangements, organized by relations of markedness, and encoded in the khipu by means of the system of binary coding.

CHAPTER 7

Conclusions

I return, finally, to the question with which I began this study: Did khipu record keeping represent a system of mnemonics? If so, bearing in mind the great range of types of mnemonic systems and devices discussed in Chapter 1, what type of memory scheme was it? Or was this instead a full-fledged writing system, capable of signing values from phonograms to logograms, as well as ideas, mythemes, and other general conventional values? Or do we, perhaps, need to come up with some other, new designation for the kind of system of record keeping represented by the khipu? Perhaps for the time being, we should simply refer to the mode of record keeping by means of the khipu as binary coding, and leave aside—until this model is tested and developed further (which I plan to do in the near future)—the question of whether or not this represents a complex form of mnemonics or a writing system. At the very least, it is hoped that we have successfully dispelled the oft-repeated comparison between khipu and rosaries and other simple memory-directing routines and devices (Figure 7.1).

Let us be perfectly clear on this one point at the end of this study: A rosary is a series of beads on a string. A message stick is a series of incisions on a stick. A khipu is an arrangement of cotton and/or wool strings—some or all of which may be dyed in astonishingly complex arrays of colors—which have been either Z-spun/S-plied or S-spun/Z-plied and attached recto or verso to a common (primary) string, and bear knots that may be (but are not necessarily) tied in a hierarchical, decimal-place fashion using three different types of knots that are tied with their primary axes either in an S- or Z-direction (Figure 7.2). In short, neither a rosary nor a message stick is even *remotely* similar to a khipu. Thus, whatever a rosary or a message stick was used for cannot be

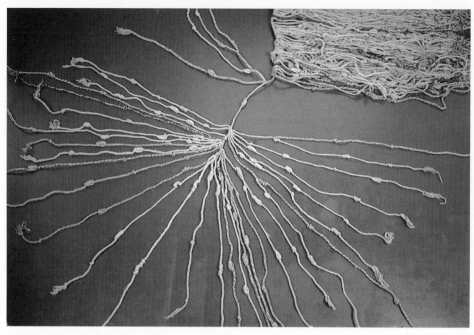

7.1. Khipu (Museum für Völkerkunde, Berlin, VA 42593).

assumed to have the least bit of relevance or precedential value whatsoever for suggesting, much less determining, *what* a khipu was used for or *how* it might have been used.

Finally, building on the important contributions of past and present-day khipu specialists (esp. Locke, Ascher and Ascher, and Conklin), this study has attempted to introduce a new form of analysis into Inka studies—that of binary coding. The central ideas and concepts that I believe have been added here to the debate over the nature of khipu record keeping are the following:

(a) an elaboration of the idea that binary coding was one of the principal mechanisms of and strategies for record keeping in the Inka khipu;

(b) a separation between the recording code and the script, or the "readable" message, in the khipu;

(c) the argument that the binary coding of khipu constituted a means for encoding paired elements that were in relationships of binary opposition to each other, and that, at a semantic level, these relations were of a character known in the literature as markedness relations; and

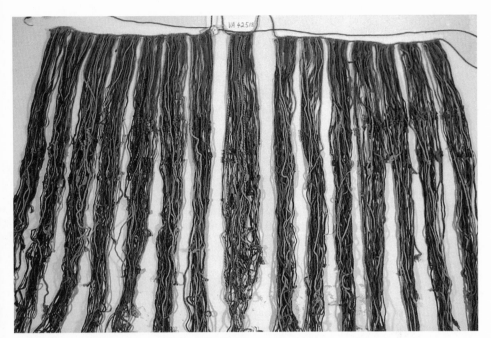

7.2. Khipu (Museum für Völkerkunde, Berlin, VA 42518).

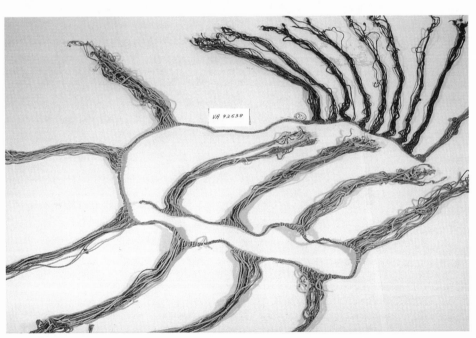

7.3. Khipu (Museum für Völkerkunde, Berlin, VA 42538).

(d) the beginnings of sketching out a theory of interpreting the hierarchical and asymmetrical (i.e., marked/unmarked) signs of, especially, nondecimal ("anomalous") khipu as the architecture for
canonical literatures (e.g., poetry, historical narratives) whose
essential components would have been noted by khipukamayuq
and used as the framework—call it mnemonic or call it a simple
number/object writing—for constructing narrative recitations.

In the future, I hope we will find this a helpful and productive model
to build on in our continuing studies of these extraordinary record-
keeping devices of the pre-Columbian and early colonial Andean worlds
(Figure 7.3).

Tabular Description of Khipu UR19 from Chachapoyas

KHIPU UR19
Museum identification: CMA-480/LC1-109.3 (Centro Mallqui,
    Leymebamba, Peru)
Material: Cotton
Main cord:
    Construction: Z-Spin/S-Ply
    Color: W
    Total length: 26.0 cm.
    $ 0.0 cm: beginning knot; space of 0.5 cm.
        0.5 cm: group of 3 pendants (1–3); space of 1.0 cm.
        2.5 cm: group of 4 pendants (4–7); space of 1.0 cm.
        4.5 cm: group of 5 pendants (8–12); space of 2.0 cm.
        7.5 cm: one pendant (13); space of 10.5 cm.
        24.0 cm: end knot ¢; space of 1.5 cm.

Pendant (spin/ply/attach.)	Knot (no./type/ position/direction)	Length	Color	Value	Subsidiaries
1 (Z/S/?)	—	0.5b	AB	—	—
2 (Z/S/v)	—	16.0b	AB	—	—
3 (Z/S/v)	1S(10.5/Z); 8L(20.0/Z)	32.0¢	AB	18	1:5.0
3s1 (Z/S)	9L(13.5/Z)	31.0	KB:W	9	—
4 (Z/S/v)	1E(20.0/S)	39.5	MB	1	—
5 (Z/S/r)	—	21.0b	AB	—	—

Pendant (spin/ply/attach.)	Knot (no./type/ position/direction)	Length	Color	Value	Subs.
6 (Z/\/?)	1S(9.5/Z)	31.0	KB	10	1:2.0
6s1 (Z/S)	(untied knot)	32.0	W	—	—
7 (Z/S/r)	1E(12.0/Z)	18.5	MB	1	1:4.0
7s1 (S/Z)	2L(8.0/Z)	13.0	KB	2	—
8 (S/Z/v)	—	40.0¢	MB	—	—
9 (S/Z/v)	2S(9.0/Z); 8L(17.0/Z)	27.0	KB:W	28	1:4.5
9s1 (S/Z)	3L(11.5/Z)	17.0¢	W	3	—
10 (S/Z/v)	2S(9.0/Z)	33.0¢	MB	20	1:2.0
10s1 (S/Z)	8L(15.5/Z)	35.0	KB:W	8	—
11 (S/Z/v)	—	49.5¢	W	—	—
12 (S/Z/v)	—	29.0¢	BL	—	—
13 (S/Z/r)	—	36.0	BL	—	—

Keys:

Main Cord Key

W	white
$	beginning knot (twisted end of main cord)
¢	end knot (on main cord and pendant strings)

Pendant Key

Z	Z-spin or -ply
S	S-spin or -ply
v	verso attachment
r	recto attachment
?	unable to determine attachment direction

(Ex.: Z/S/v = Z-spun/S-plied/verso-attached pendant string)

Knot Key

S	single knot
L	long knot
E	figure-eight knot
S	S-knot
Z	Z-knot

(Ex.: 2S(9.0Z) = two single knots tied at 9.0 cm from the attachment of the pendant string to main cord, both tied as Z-knots)

Length Key

b	broken string
¢	end knot
absence of b and ¢	no end knot; not broken

(Ex.: 0.5b = 0.5 cm broken pendant string)

Color Key

AB	light brown
BL	pale blue
MB	moderate brown
KB	dark brown
W	white
:	mottled (i.e., two colors mixed together)

(Ex.: KB:W = dark brown and white mottled string)

Value Key
Decimal reading of knots

(Ex.: 28 = two single knots in 10s position + long knot of eight)

Subsidiary Key
Number of subsidiaries followed by location on pendant string

(Ex.: 1:2.0 = one subsidiary tied to pendant string at 2.0 cm from attachment of pendant string to main cord)

Notes

1. Memory, Writing, and Record Keeping in the Inka Empire

1. The spelling of Quechua words in this book will generally follow the orthographic conventions used in Antonio Cusihuamán's *Diccionario Quechua Cuzco-Collao* (1976). For instance, rather than the Hispanicized forms *quipu* and *quipucamayoq*, I use the phonologically more accurate forms *khipu* and *khipukamayuq*. Hispanicized terms in colonial quotations are left in their original forms.

2. In referring to the string structures of khipu, I prefer to use descriptive and functional nomenclature (i.e., primary cord, pendant string, and subsidiaries). These terms are equivalent to Conklin's more structural designations: (respectively) primary, secondary, and tertiary strings (see Conklin 2002).

3. For a similar argument concerning the invention and development of complexity in numbering and mathematical systems, see Urton 1997: 132–137.

4. This is reminiscent of the information provided by the Peruvian anthropologist Oscar Núñez del Prado on the khipu that were in use in the 1950s in Paucartambo, Dept. of Cusco. He found that in many communities, herders who kept records of hacienda livestock had *paired* khipu; one contained information pertaining to the composition of the herd, organized by categories of animals (e.g., reproductive females, males capable of breeding, etc.), and the other contained totals. The purpose of the pairing of khipu was to provide a means for checking records (Núñez del Prado 1990).

5. Another student of the khipu, William Burns (2001: 30–31), has suggested that the number words (in Quechua) designating the quantitative values tied into strings encoded phonological values that were used in some way to write in a system of syllabograms. Although this is an intriguing suggestion, Burns has not produced any readings of "texts" using this approach. In addition, Burns's interpretation does not account for any of the other forms of variation and patterning in the khipu (e.g., spinning, plying, attachment, and knotting directionality; see Chapter 3). Thus, this interpretation, as well as that of the Aschers (i.e., the notion of "number labels"), leaves completely unmotivated and uninterpreted the majority of information recorded on the khipu.

2. Theory and Methods in the Study of Khipu Binary Coding

1. To say that the Inka did not produce a graphic script is not to say that they could not produce geometrical and other images in graphemic forms, for they did precisely this, both in their woven geometrical *tuqapu* designs (see Arellano 1999; Rowe 1997) and in the painted and engraved designs on their ritual drinking vessels, the *keros* (see Cummins 1988). Frank Salomon (2001) has also produced an incisive and highly relevant study for consideration in regard to the uses and significance of graphemes in the (contemporary) Andes. Salomon's study concerns the annual inscription and display of a standard set of graphemes inscribed on ceremonial staffs of office (*varas*) in the community of Tupicocha, east of Lima.

2. I note that a kernel of the theory of binary coding elaborated in this study was suggested in a work published several years ago by Marcia Ascher: "When considering the possible uses of a system restricted to digits variously assorted [like the khipu], one needs only remember that digital computers store only strings of 1's and 0's. We impute different meanings to different collections of them and thereby store, process, and retrieve a variety of numeric and non-numeric information" (1986: 282–283).

3. The Aschers' *Databooks* have recently become available on-line at: http://instruct1.cit.cornell.edu/research/quipu-ascher/.

3. The Physical Components of Khipu Binary Coding

1. For a description and analysis of different spinning procedures and practices in the Andes, see Dransart 1995; Frame 2001; Goodell 1969; and Oakland 1982.

2. The khipu from the Chachapoyas region were discovered—along with some 220 well-preserved mummy bundles—in a set of a half-dozen burial chambers (*chullpas*) built into a rock overhang in a cliff face overlooking a lake called Laguna de los Cóndores (Lake of the Condors; see Lerche 1999; von Hagen and Guillén 1998). I am currently at work on a book-length study of these khipu (see Urton 2001).

3. I developed the pendant-attachment nomenclature *recto/verso* while working in the field on the Chachapoya khipu. After I had completed this work, and had already recorded my tabular data for the khipu in Table 1 using this terminology, I realized that Conklin (2002) had employed a different nomenclature for these two forms of string attachment. The terms employed by Conklin are: "reverse" (= recto) and "front/obverse" (= verso).

4. As I stated in Chapter 2, in designating khipu in the collection from Chachapoyas with labels beginning "UR" (= Urton), I am following the convention established by the pioneers of khipu documentary studies, Marcia and Robert Ascher (see especially Ascher and Ascher 1978). Each khipu studied by the Aschers is designated in their reports by an "AS" (= Ascher) number, thereby indicating to later researchers the source(s) of measurements and observations made on the khipu samples in question. The museum identification numbers

in the Centro Mallqui collections, Leymebamba, Peru, of the two khipu in question here are: CMA-628/LC1-257B (= UR2), and CMA-480/LC1-109.2 (= UR5).

5. The existence of variations in knot directionality in the khipu was first pointed out to me by Bill Conklin. This was during a day-long informal study that we undertook jointly of the ca. 100 samples in the American Museum of Natural History, New York, on February 28, 1992. To the best of my knowledge, Bill Conklin was also the first to designate the two variations in knot directionality as Z- and S-knots. However, the formal definitions and descriptions of the forms of these two knotting variations as they appear in the three knot types given in this book are based on my own study and observations of the khipu in the Museum für Völkerkunde, Berlin, in June 1993.

6. Khipu collections on whose study these observations are based include the Museum für Völkerkunde, Berlin (ca. 298 samples); the American Museum of Natural History, New York (ca. 100 samples); the Peabody Museum of Archaeology and Ethnology, Cambridge, Mass. (13 samples); and the Centro Mallqui, Leymebamba, Peru (32 samples). Of the total of approximately 443 khipu studied, data could not be recorded for some 50–75, due to the extreme fragility of these specimens.

7. This khipu is in the collections of the Museum für Völkerkunde in Berlin. The museum accession number is VA 42527. The number assigned to this sample in the Aschers' study of khipu in this collection is AS 104 (see Ascher and Ascher 1978).

4. The Linguistic Components of Khipu Binary Coding

1. Khipu B/8705 was studied earlier in this century by Locke, who published a full reading of the knot values on all 153 strings and subsidiaries of this khipu (Locke 1928). Locke published his readings in a "working paper," in which he first made the information on this and several other khipu available for study. Curiously, Locke begins his recording of the values on Khipu B/8705 by reasserting his conclusion, from one of his earlier publications (1923), that khipu record numerical values in a base-ten system of numeration. However, when one looks at Locke's transcription of Khipu B/8705, it is clear that this particular sample completely violates the fundamental patterns of knot-type placement and other decimal organizational principles that he had identified for khipu in general.

5. Khipu Sign Capacity and Code Conversion

1. See William Conklin's (2002) discussion of the storage capacity of khipu, in which he takes a different approach but similarly concludes that the khipu had substantial information storage capacity.

2. For a particularly comprehensive and clear discussion of the evolution of Chinese characters from an early (Shang) period form of primarily pictographic and logographic signs to the predominantly semantic-phonetic signs used from the eighteenth century to the present, see DeFrancis 1989: 97–99.

3. ". . . i los Quipo Camayos, ya por los privilegios con que les onrava el oficio, ya porque si no davan razón de lo que se les preguntava tenían grandes castigos, i así estavan continuamente estudiando en las señales, cifras i relaciones, enseñándoselas a los que les avían de suceder en los oficios, i avía número destos Secretarios, que cada qual tenía repartido su género de materia, aviendo de corresponder el cuento, relación, o cantar a los ñudos que servían de índice, i punto para memoria local" (Calancha 1974: 205).

4. "Fuera de estos quipos de hilo tienen otros de pedrezuelas, por donde puntualmente aprenden las palabras que quieren tomar de memoria, y es cosa de ver a viejos ya caducos con una rueda hecha de pedrezuelas aprender el Padrenuestro, y con otra el Avemaría, y con otra el Credo, y saber cuál piedra es: que fué concebido de Espíritu Santo, y cuál; que padeció debajo del poder de Poncio Pilato, y no hay más que verlos enmendar cuando yerran, y toda la enmienda consiste en mirar sus pedrezuelas, que a mí, para hacerme olvidar cuanto sé de coro, me bastará una rueda de aquéllas.

"De éstas suele haber no pocas en los cimenterios de las iglesias, para este efecto; pues verles otra suerte de quipos que usan de granos de maíz, es cosa que encanta; porque una cuenta muy buen contador que hacer por pluma y tinta, para ver a cómo les cabe entre tantos, tanto de contribución, sacando tanto de acullá y añadiendo tanto de acá, con otras cien retartalillas, tomarán estos indios sus granos y pornán uno aquí, tres acullá, ocho no sé dónde; pasarán un grano de aquí, trocarán tres de acullá, y, en efecto, ellos salen con su cuenta hecha puntualísimamente sin errar un tilde, y mucho mejor se saben ellos poner en cuenta y razón de lo que cabe a cada uno de pagar o dar, que sabremos nosotros dárselo por pluma y tinta averiguado. Si esto no es íngenio y si estos hombres son bestias, júzguelo quien quisiere, que lo que yo juzgo de cierto es que, en aquello que se aplican, nos hacen grandes ventajas" (Acosta 1954: 190).

5. I myself plan to apply this methodology in a large-scale, computer-based study of khipu samples in the near future.

6. Khipu UR19 carries the Centro Mallqui catalog number CMA480/LCI-109.3. This is one of a total of seven Chachapoya khipu that were found tied together and deposited in the burial chambers at Laguna de los Cóndores (see Guillén 1999; Urton 2001; von Hagen 2000).

6. Sign Theory, Markedness, and Parallelism in the Khipu Information System

1. I have hedged on this point because, from my fieldwork in Pacariqtambo, Peru, in the 1980s, I am in fact aware of cases in which individuals can be considered to belong to both of the moieties of the community (*hanansayaq* and *hurinsayaq*), depending on the context of evaluation or attribution. For instance, one may belong to one of the moieties by virtue of being the descendant of a male member of that moiety; however, if one buys land traditionally belonging to the opposite moiety (which is theoretically not allowed!), one will be pressed into service to help sponsor a festival that is the ritual obligation of an *ayllu* of that moiety (see Urton 1990).

2. Lydia Fossa (2000) makes an interesting and relevant argument in this regard. She suggests that the two khipukamayuq who testified concerning tribute payments in the legal proceeding of the 1590s between the Sacaca Indians of central Bolivia and Alonso de Montemayor (Platt 2002; Urton 1998) may, in fact, have retained the two parts of a *moiety*-based tribute accounting.

Bibliography

Acosta, José de
1954   *Historia natural y moral de las Indias.* In *Obras del P. José de Acosta,*
[1590] edited by P. Francisco Mateos. Biblioteca de Autores Españoles,
        vol. 73. Madrid: Ediciones Atlas.

Adorno, Rolena
1998   "Criterios de comprobación: El manuscrito Miccinelli de Nápoles y
        las crónicas de la conquista del Perú." *Antropologica* 16: N.p.

Almeder, Robert
1980   *The Philosophy of Charles S. Peirce: A Critical Introduction.* Totowa,
        N.J.: Rowman and Littlefield.

Andrews, Edna
1990   *Markedness Theory: The Union of Asymmetry and Semiosis in Language.*
        Durham and London: Duke University Press.

Animato, Carlo, Paolo A. Rossi, and Clara Miccinelli
1989   *Quipu: Il nodo parlante dei misteriosi Incas.* Genoa: Edizioni Culturali
        Internazionali.

Ansión, Juan
1990   "Cómo calculaban los incas." In *Quipu y yupana,* edited by Carol
        Mackey et al., 257–266. Lima: Consejo Nacional de Ciencias y
        Tecnología.

Arellano, Carmen
1999   "Quipu y tocapu: Sistemas de comunicación incas." In *Los incas: Arte
        y símbolos,* edited by Franklin Pease et al., 215–261. Colección Arte y
        Tesoros del Perú. Lima: Banco de Crédito del Perú.

Arnold, Denise Y., and Juan de Dios Yapita
2000   *El rincón de las cabezas: Luchas textuales, educación y tierras en los Andes.*
        Colección Academia, no. 9. La Paz: STAMPA Gráfica Digital.

Ascher, Marcia
1986   "Mathematical Ideas of the Incas." In *Native American Mathematics,*
        edited by Michael P. Closs, 261–289. Austin: University of Texas
        Press.

1991   *Ethnomathematics: A Multicultural View of Mathematical Ideas.* Pacific
        Grove, Calif.: Brooks/Cole.
2002   "Reading Khipu: Labels, Structure, and Format." In *Narrative
        Threads: Accounting and Recounting in Andean Khipu,* edited by
        Jeffrey Quilter and Gary Urton, 87–102. Austin: University of Texas
        Press.

Ascher, Marcia, and Robert Ascher
1969   "Code of Ancient Peruvian Knotted Cords (Quipus)." *Nature* 222:
        529–533.
1975   "The Quipu as a Visible Language." *Visible Language* 9, no. 4: 329–
        356.
1978   *Code of the Quipu: Databooks I and II.* Available upon request from
        Cornell University Archives, Ithaca, N.Y.
1997   *Code of the Quipu.* New York: Dover Publications.
[1981]

Ascher, Robert
2002   "Inca Writing." In *Narrative Threads: Accounting and Recounting in
        Andean Khipu,* edited by Jeffrey Quilter and Gary Urton, 103–118.
        Austin: University of Texas Press.

Aveni, Anthony F.
1986   "Non-Western Notational Frameworks and the Role of Anthro-
        pology in Our Understanding of Literacy." In *Toward a New Under-
        standing of Literacy,* edited by Merald E. Wrolstad and Dennis F.
        Fisher, 252–280. New York: Praeger.

Battistella, Edwin L.
1996   *The Logic of Markedness.* New York and Oxford: Oxford University
        Press.

Bauer, Brian S.
1997   "The Original *Ceque* Manuscript." In *Structure, Knowledge, and Repre-
        sentation in the Andes. Vol. 2: Studies Presented to Reiner Tom Zuidema
        on the Occasion of His 70th Birthday. Journal of the Steward Anthropo-
        logical Society* 25, nos. 1 and 2: 277–298.

Bertonio, Ludovico
1984   *Vocabulario de la Lengua Aymara.* Cochabamba, Bolivia: Ediciones
[1612] CERES.

Birket-Smith, Kaj
1966–   "The Circumpacific Distribution of Knot Records." *Folk* 8/9: 15–24.
1967

Boone, Elizabeth H.
1994   "Introduction: Writing and Recording Knowledge." In *Writing with-
        out Words: Alternative Literacies in Mesoamerica and the Andes,* edited
        by Elizabeth H. Boone and Walter D. Mignolo, 3–26. Durham and
        London: Duke University Press.

Boone, Elizabeth H., and Walter D. Mignolo, eds.
1994   *Writing without Words: Alternative Literacies in Mesoamerica and the Andes.* Durham and London: Duke University Press.

Bourdieu, Pierre
1979   *Outline of a Theory of Practice.* Cambridge: Cambridge University Press.

Brent, Joseph
1993   *Charles Sanders Peirce: A Life.* Bloomington and Indianapolis: Indiana University Press.

Brokaw, Galen
1999   "Transcultural Intertextuality and Quipu Literacy in Felipe Guaman Poma de Ayala's *Nueva corónica y buen gobierno.*" Ph.D. dissertation, Indiana University. Ann Arbor: UMI Dissertation Services.

Burns Glynn, William
1987   *Los kipus como escritura fonética de los inkas.* Chicago: Northwest Premier Printing.

Calancha, Antonio de la
1974   *Crónica moralizada del orden de San Agustín en el Perú con sucesos ejem-*
[1638] *plares en esta monarquía.* Vol. 1. Transcripción, estudio crítico, notas bibliográficas e índices de Ignacio Prado Pastor. Lima: Universidad Nacional Mayor de San Marcos.

Callapiña, Supno, and Other Khipukamayuq
1974   *Relación de la descendencia, gobierno y conquista de los incas.* Prologue by
[1542/ Juan José Vega. Lima: Ediciones de la Biblioteca Universitaria.
1608]

Cañizares-Esguerra, Jorge
2001   *How to Write the History of the New World: Histories, Epistemologies, and Identities in the Eighteenth-Century Atlantic World.* Stanford: Stanford University Press.

Cantù, Francesca, ed.
2001   *Guaman Poma y Blas Valera: Tradición andina e historia colonial.* Actas del Coloquio Internacional, Instituto Italo-Latinoamericano, Rome, September 29–30, 1999. Rome: Antonio Pellicani Editore.

Carruthers, Mary
1993   *The Book of Memory: A Study of Memory in Medieval Culture.* Cambridge: Cambridge University Press.

Caton, Steven C.
1987   "Contributions to Roman Jakobson." *Annual Review of Anthropology* 16: 223–260.

Cereceda, Verónica
1986   "The Semiology of Andean Textiles: The Talegas of Isluga." In

Anthropological History of Andean Polities, edited by John V. Murra, Nathan Wachtel, and Jacques Revel, 149–174. Cambridge: Cambridge University Press.

1990   "A partir de los colores de un pájaro." *Boletín del Museo Chileno de Arte Pre-colombino* 4: 57–104.

Chadwick, John
1994   *The Mycenaean World.* Cambridge: Cambridge University Press.
[1976]

Classen, Constance
1993   *Inca Cosmology and the Human Body.* Salt Lake City: University of Utah Press.

Cobo, Bernabé
1964   *Obras del P. Bernabé Cobo.* Vol. 1. Edited and preliminary study by P. Francisco Mateos. Biblioteca de Autores Españoles, vol. 91. Madrid: Ediciones Atlas.

1983   *History of the Inca Empire.* Translated and edited by Roland Hamilton.
[1653]   Austin: University of Texas Press.

Coe, Michael D.
1995   *Breaking the Maya Code.* New York: Thames and Hudson.

Coe, Michael D., and Mark van Stone
2001   *Reading the Maya Glyphs.* London: Thames and Hudson.

Conklin, William J
1982   "The Information System of the Middle Horizon Quipus." In *Ethnoastronomy and Archaeoastronomy in the American Tropics,* edited by Anthony F. Aveni and Gary Urton, 261–281. Annals of the New York Academy of Sciences, vol. 385. New York: New York Academy of Sciences.

2002   "A Khipu Information String Theory." In *Narrative Threads: Accounting and Recounting in Andean Khipu,* edited by Jeffrey Quilter and Gary Urton, 53–86. Austin: University of Texas Press.

Connerton, Paul
1989   *How Societies Remember.* Cambridge: Cambridge University Press.

Cooper, Jerrold S.
1996   "Sumerian and Akkadian." In *The World's Writing Systems,* edited by Peter T. Daniels and William Bright, 37–56. New York and Oxford: Oxford University Press.

Coulmas, Florian
1992   *The Writing Systems of the World.* Oxford, England, and Cambridge, Mass.: Blackwell.

Coulmas, Florian, and Konrad Ehlich, eds.
1983   *Writing in Focus.* Trends in Linguistics: Studies and Monographs

No. 24; Werner Winter, series editor. Berlin, New York, and Amsterdam: Mouton.

Cummins, Thomas B. F.
1988   *Abstraction to Narration: Kero Imagery of Peru and the Colonial Alteration of Native Identity.* Ph.D. dissertation, University of California, Los Angeles. Ann Arbor: University Microfilms.

Cusihuamán, Antonio
1976   *Gramática Quechua Cuzco-Collao.* Lima: Instituto de Estudios Peruanos.

D'Altroy, Terence N.
2002   *The Incas.* Malden, Mass., and Oxford: Basil Blackwell.

Daniels, Peter T., and William Bright, eds.
1996   "The Invention of Writing." In *The World's Writing Systems,* edited by Peter T. Daniels and William Bright, 577–586. New York and Oxford: Oxford University Press.

Dávalos, Johnny, Verónica Cereceda, and Gabriel Martínez
1994   *Textiles Tarabuco.* 2d ed. Sucre, Bolivia: Ediciones ASUR 2.

de Certeau, Michel
1984   *The Practice of Everyday Life.* Berkeley and Los Angeles: University of California Press.

DeFrancis, John
1989   *Visible Speech: The Diverse Oneness of Writing Systems.* Honolulu: University of Hawaii Press.

Deledalle, Gérard
2000   *Charles S. Peirce's Philosophy of Signs: Essays in Comparative Semiotics.* Bloomington and Indianapolis: Indiana University Press.

Domenici, Viviano, and Davide Domenici
1996   "Talking Knots of the Inka." *Archaeology* 49, no. 6 (November/December): 50–56.

Drake, Stillman
1986   "Literacy and Scientific Notations." In *Toward a New Understanding of Literacy,* edited by Merald E. Wrolstad and Dennis F. Fisher, 135–155. New York: Praeger.

Dransart, Penny
1995   "Inner Worlds and the Event of a Thread in Isluga, Northern Chile." In *Andean Art: Visual Expression and Its Relation to Andean Beliefs and Values,* edited by Penny Dransart, 228–242. Avebury: Ashgate Publishing.

Eck, David J.
1995   *The Most Complex Machine: A Survey of Computers and Computing.* Wellesley, Mass.: A. K. Peters.

Eco, Umberto
1977   "The Influence of Roman Jakobson on the Development of Semi-
        otics." In *Roman Jakobson: Echoes of His Scholarship,* edited by Daniel
        Armstrong and C. H. van Schooneveld, 39–56. Lisse, The Nether-
        lands: Peter de Ridder Press.

Fentress, James, and Chris Wickham
1992   *Social Memory.* Oxford, England, and Cambridge, Mass.: Blackwell.

Flores Ochoa, Jorge A.
1986   "The Classification and Naming of South American Camelids." In
        Anthropological History of Andean Polities, edited by John V. Murra,
        Nathan Wachtel, and Jacques Revel, 137–148. Cambridge: Cam-
        bridge University Press.

Fossa, Lydia
2000   "Two Khipu, One Narrative: Answering Urton's Questions." *Ethno-
        history* 47, no. 2: 453–468.

Fox, James J.
1974   "'Our Ancestors Spoke in Pairs': Rotinese Views of Language, Dia-
        lect, and Code." In *Explorations in the Ethnography of Speaking,* edited
        by Richard Bauman and Joel Sherzer, 65–85. Cambridge: Cambridge
        University Press.
1975   "On Binary Categories and Primary Symbols: Some Rotinese Per-
        spectives." In *The Interpretation of Symbolism,* edited by Roy Willis,
        99–132. New York: John Wiley and Sons.
1977   "Roman Jakobson and the Comparative Study of Parallelism." In *Ro-
        man Jakobson: Echoes of His Scholarship,* edited by Daniel Armstrong
        and C. H. van Schooneveld, 59–90. Lisse, The Netherlands: Peter de
        Ridder Press.
1988   *To Speak in Pairs: Essays on the Ritual Languages of Eastern Indonesia.*
        Cambridge: Cambridge University Press.

Frame, Mary
2001   "Beyond the Image: The Dimensions of Pattern in Ancient Andean
        Textiles." In *Abstraction: The Amerindian Paradigm,* edited by César
        Paternosto, 113–136. Brussels: Société des Expositions du Palais des
        Beaux-Arts de Bruxelles.

Garcilaso de la Vega
1966   *Royal Commentaries of the Incas.* 2 vols. Translated and with an intro-
[1609– duction by Harold V. Livermore. Austin: University of Texas Press.
1617]

Gelb, I. J.
1963   *A Study of Writing.* Chicago: University of Chicago Press.
[1952]

Giddens, Anthony
1983   *Central Problems in Social Theory: Action, Structure, and Contradiction*

in Social Analysis. Berkeley and Los Angeles: University of California Press.

Goodell, Grace
1969   "A Study of Andean Spinning in the Cuzco Region." *The Textile Museum Journal* 11, no. 3: 2–8.

Goodman, Nelson
1976   *Languages of Art: An Approach to a Theory of Symbols.* Indianapolis: Hackett Publishing.

Gose, Peter
1996   "The Past Is a Lower Moiety: Diarchy, History, and Divine Kingship in the Inka Empire." *History and Anthropology* 9, no 4: 383–414.

Gossen, Gary H.
1974   *Chamulas in the World of the Sun.* Cambridge: Harvard University Press.

Gragg, Gene B.
1996   "Other Languages." In *The World's Writing Systems,* edited by Peter T. Daniels and William Bright, 58–72. New York and Oxford: Oxford University Press.

Greenberg, Joseph
1966   *Language Universals.* The Hague: Mouton.
1977   *A New Invitation to Linguistics.* Garden City, N.J.: Anchor Press/ Doubleday.

Guaman Poma de Ayala, Felipe
1980   *El primer nueva corónica y buen gobierno.* Critical edition by John V.
[1615] Murra and Rolena Adorno; translation and textual analysis by Jorge L. Urioste. 3 vols. Mexico City: Siglo Veintiuno.

Guillén, Sonia E.
1999   "Arqueología de emergencia: Inventario, catalogación y conservación de los materiales arqueológicos de los mausoleos de la Laguna de los Cóndores." Final report to the Instituto Nacional de Cultura, Lima.

Haas, W., ed.
1976   *Writing without Letters.* Manchester, England: Manchester University Press.

Halbwachs, Maurice
1992   *On Collective Memory.* Chicago and London: University of Chicago
[1941/ Press.
1952]

Harris, Roy
1986   *The Origin of Writing.* LaSalle, Ill.: Open Court.
1995   *Signs of Writing.* London and New York: Routledge.

Hasenohr, Geneviève
1982   "Méditation méthodique et mnémonique: Un témoignage figuré
         ancien (XIIIe–XIVe S.)" In *Clio et son regard: Mélanges d'histoire,
         d'histoire de l'art et d'archéologie offerts à Jacques Stiennon,* edited by
         Rita Jejeune and Joseph Deckers, 365–382. Liège: Pierre Mardaga.

Hertz, Robert
1973   "The Preeminence of the Right Hand: A Study in Religious Polarity."
         In *Right and Left: Essays on Dual Symbolic Classification,* edited by
         Rodney Needham, 3–35. Cambridge: Cambridge University Press.

Holenstein, Elmar
1974   *Roman Jakobson's Approach to Language: Phenomenological Struc-
         turalism.* Translated by Catherine Schelbert and Tarcisius Schelbert.
         Bloomington and London: Indiana University Press.

Holisky, Dee Ann
1996   "The Georgian Alphabet." In *The World's Writing Systems,* edited
         by Peter T. Daniels and William Bright, 364–369. New York and
         Oxford: Oxford University Press.

Holm, Olaf
1968   "Quipu o sapan: Un recurso mnemónico en el campo ecuatoriano."
         Cuadernos de Historia y Arqueología 18, nos. 34–35: 85–90.

Hoskins, Janet
1998   *Biographical Objects: How Things Tell the Stories of People's Lives.* New
         York and London: Routledge.

Houston, Stephen D.
1996   *Maya Glyphs.* Berkeley and Los Angeles: University of California
[1989]   Press.

Howard, Rosaleen (see also Howard-Malverde, R.)
2002   "Spinning a Yarn: Landscape, Memory, and Discourse Structure
         in Quechua Narratives." In *Narrative Threads: Accounting and Re-
         counting in Andean Khipu,* edited by Jeffrey Quilter and Gary Urton,
         26–49. Austin: University of Texas Press.

Howard-Malverde, Rosaleen (see also Howard, R.)
1990   *The Speaking of History: 'Willapaakushayki,' or Quechua Ways of Telling
         the Past.* University of London, Institute of Latin American Studies
         Research Papers No. 21. London: Institute of Latin American
         Studies.

Hutton, Patrick H.
1993   *History as an Art of Memory.* Hanover, N.H., and London: University
         Press of New England.

Hyland, Sabine
2002   "Woven Words." In *Narrative Threads: Accounting and Recounting in*

Andean Khipu, edited by Jeffrey Quilter and Gary Urton, 152–170. Austin: University of Texas Press.

Isbell, Billie Jean
1985   "The Metaphoric Process: 'From Nature to Culture and Back Again.'" In *Animal Myths and Metaphors in South America,* edited by Gary Urton, 285–313. Salt Lake City: University of Utah Press.

Iversen, Erik
1993   *The Myth of Egypt and Its Hieroglyphs in European Tradition.* Prince-
[1961] ton, N.J.: Princeton University Press.

Jakobson, Roman
1960   "Linguistics and Poetics." In *Language in Literature,* edited by Krystyna Pomorska and Stephen Rudy, 62–94. Cambridge: Cambridge University Press.
1966   "Grammatical Parallelism and Its Russian Facet." In *Language in Literature,* edited by Krystyna Pomorska and Stephen Rudy, 145–179. Cambridge: Cambridge University Press.
1985   *Verbal Art, Verbal Sign, Verbal Time.* Edited by Krystyna Pomorska and Stephen Rudy. Oxford: Basil Blackwell.

Johansen, Jørgen Dines
1993   *Dialogic Semiosis: An Essay on Signs and Meanings.* Bloomington and Indianapolis: Indiana University Press.

Julien, Catherine J.
1988   "How Inca Decimal Administration Worked." *Ethnohistory* 35, no. 3: 257–279.
2000   *Reading Inca History.* Iowa City: University of Iowa Press.

Kaulicke, Peter
2000   *Memoria y muerte en el Perú antiguo.* Lima: Pontificia Universidad Católica del Perú.

Kiefer, Ferenc
1989   "Towards a Theory of Semantic Markedness." In *Markedness in Synchrony and Diachrony,* edited by O. M. Tomic, 121–138. Berlin and New York: Mouton de Gruyter.

Laurencich Minelli, Laura
1996   *La scrittura dell'antico Perù: Un mondo da scoprire.* Biblioteca di scienze umane, No. 5. Bologna, Italy: Clueb Lexis.
1999a   "La 'culpa' del cronista peruano P. Blas Valera." *Anales, Museo de América* 7: 95–109.
1999b   "Un complemento a la polémica sobre Guaman Poma de Ayala." *Antropologica* 17: 422–427.
2001   *Il linguaggio magico-religioso dei numeri, dei fili e della musica presso gli Inca.* Bologna: Società Editrice Esculapio.

Lave, Jean, and Etienne Wenger
1991   *Situated Learning: Legitimate Peripheral Participation.* Cambridge:
         Cambridge University Press.

Lerche, Peter
1999   "A Grave Case of Robbery." *Geographical* 71, no. 5: 18–23.

Liszka, James Jakób
1996   *A General Introduction to the Semeiotic of Charles Sanders Peirce.*
         Bloomington and Indianapolis: Indiana University Press.

Locke, L. Leland
1912   "The Ancient Quipu, A Peruvian Knot Record," *American Anthro-
         pologist* 14: 325–332.
1923   *The Ancient Quipu or Peruvian Knot Record.* New York: American
         Museum of Natural History.
1928   "Supplementary Notes on the Quipus in the American Museum of
         Natural History." Anthropological Papers of the American Museum
         of Natural History, Vol. 30, Part 2: 37–71. New York: American
         Museum of Natural History.

Lord, Albert B.
1960   *The Singer of Tales.* Harvard Studies in Comparative Literature
         No. 24. Cambridge: Harvard University Press.

Loza, Carmen Beatriz
1998   "Du bon usage des quipus face à l'administration coloniale espagnole,
         1553–1599." *Population* 53, no. 2: 139–160.

MacCormack, Sabine
1995   "'En los tiempos muy antiguos . . .': Cómo se recordaba el pasado
         en el Perú de la colonía temprana." *Revista Ecuatoriana de Historia* 7:
         3–33.
2001   "History, Historical Record, and Ceremonial Action: Incas and
         Spaniards in Cuzco." *Comparative Studies in Society and History* 43,
         no. 2: 329–363.

Mackey, Carol
1970   *Knot Records in Ancient and Modern Peru.* Ph.D. dissertation, Univer-
         sity of California, Berkeley. Ann Arbor: University Microfilms.
2002   "The Continuing Khipu Traditions: Principles and Practices." In *Nar-
         rative Threads: Accounting and Recounting in Andean Khipu,* edited
         by Jeffrey Quilter and Gary Urton, 320–347. Austin: University of
         Texas Press.

Mackey, Carol, Hugo Pereyra, Carlos Radicati, Humberto Rodríguez, and
Oscar Valverde, eds.
1990   *Quipu y yupana: Colección de escritos.* Lima: Consejo Nacional de
         Ciencia y Tecnología.

Mair, Victor H.
1996   "Modern Chinese Writing." In *The World's Writing Systems,* edited
        by Peter T. Daniels and William Bright, 200–208. New York and
        Oxford: Oxford University Press.

Manetti, Giovanni
1993   *Theories of the Sign in Classical Antiquity.* Translated from the Italian
[1987] by Christine Richardson. Bloomington and Indianapolis: Indiana
        University Press.

Mannheim, Bruce
1986   "Popular Song and Popular Grammar, Poetry, and Metalanguage."
        Word 37: 45–75.
1991   *The Language of the Inka since the European Invasion.* Austin: Univer-
        sity of Texas Press.
1998   "'Time, Not the Syllables, Must Be Counted': Quechua Parallel-
        ism, Word Meaning, and Cultural Analysis." *Michigan Discussions in
        Anthropology* 13: 245–287.

Matienzo, Juan de
1967   *Gobierno del Perú.* Travaux de l'Institut Français d'Etudes Andines 11.
[1567] Paris: Pierre André.

Menninger, Karl
1977   *Number Words and Number Symbols.* Cambridge, Mass., and London,
[1958] England: M.I.T. Press.

Mesa, José de, and Teresa Gisbert
1966   "Los Chipayas." *Anuario de Estudios Americanos* 23: 479–506.

Mignolo, Walter D.
1995   *The Darker Side of the Renaissance: Literacy, Territoriality, and Coloni-
        zation.* Ann Arbor: University of Michigan Press.

Minar, C. Jill
2000   "Spinning and Plying: Anthropological Directions." In *Beyond Cloth
        and Cordage: Archaeological Textile Research in the Americas,* edited by
        Penelope B. Drooker and Laurie D. Webster, 85–100. Salt Lake City:
        University of Utah Press.

Mitchell, W. J. Thomas
1987   *Iconology: Image, Text, Ideology.* Chicago and London: University of
        Chicago Press.

Molina, Cristóbal de ("el Cuzqueño")
1916   *Relación de las fábulas y ritos de los incas.* Edited by Horacio H. Urteaga
[1573] and Carlos A. Romero. Colección de Libros y Documentos Refe-
        rentes a la Historia del Perú, vol. 1. Lima: Sanmartí.

Murra, John V.
1962   "Cloth and Its Functions in the Inca State." *American Anthropologist*
        64, no. 4: 710–727.

1975   "Las etno-categorías de un *khipu* estatal." In *Formaciones económicas y políticas en el mundo andino,* 243–254. Lima: Instituto de Estudios Andinos.

Murúa, Martín de
1946   *Los orígenes de los inkas.* Edited by Raúl Porras Barrenechea. Los
[1590]   Pequeños Grandes Libros de Historia Americana, series 1, vol. 11. Lima: Imprenta Miranda.

Nissen, Hans J., Peter Damerow, and Robert K. Englund
1993   *Archaic Bookkeeping: Early Writing and Techniques of Economic Administration in the Ancient Near East.* Chicago and London: University of Chicago Press.

Nordenskiöld, Erland
1925a   "The Secret of the Peruvian Quipus." In *Comparative Ethnological Studies,* Vol. 6, Part 1. Göteborg, Sweden: Erlanders.
1925b   "Calculations with Years and Months in the Peruvian Quipus." In *Comparative Ethnological Studies,* Vol. 6, Part 2. Göteborg, Sweden: Erlanders.

Notopoulos, James A.
1938   "Mnemosyne in Oral Literature." In *Transactions and Proceedings of the American Philological Association,* edited by George D. Hadzsits, vol. 69: 465–493.

Núñez del Prado, Oscar
1990   "El kipu moderno." In *Quipu y yupana: Colección de escritos,* edited by
[1950]   Carol Mackey et al., 165–182. Lima: Consejo Nacional de Ciencia y Tecnología.

Oakland, Amy S.
1982   "Pre-Columbian Spinning and *Lloq'e* Yarn: An Ethnographic Analogy." In *Andean Perspectives Newsletter* 4: 25–30. Institute of Latin American Studies and Dept. of Anthropology, University of Texas, Austin.

Ong, Walter J.
1995   *Orality and Literacy: The Technologizing of the Word.* London and New
[1982]   York: Routledge.

Ossio, Juan M.
2000   "Nota sobre el Coloquio Internacional 'Guaman Poma de Ayala y Blas Valera: Tradición andina e historia colonial.' Instituto Italo-Latinoamericano, Roma, 29–30 de septiembre de 1999." *Colonial Latin American Review* 9, no. 1: 113–116.

Palomino Flores, Salvador
1970   "El sistema de oposiciones en la comunidad sarhua." Thesis for the Bachiller in Ciencias Antropológicas, Universidad Nacional de San Cristóbal de Huamanga, Ayacucho, Peru.

Pärssinen, Martti
1992   *Tawantinsuyu: The Inca State and Its Political Organization.* Studia
         Historica 43. Helsinki: Societas Historica Finlandiae.

Paul, Anne
1990   "The Use of Color in Paracas Necropolis Fabrics: What Does It Re-
         veal about the Organization of Dyeing, Designing, and Society?"
         National Geographic Research 6, no. 1: 7–21.

Peirce, Charles S.
1955   *Philosophical Writings of Peirce.* Selected and edited with an introduc-
[1940]   tion by Justus Buchler. New York: Dover Publications.

Pereyra S., Hugo
1990   "La yupana, complemento operacional del quipu." In *Quipu y yupana,*
         edited by Carol Mackey et al., 235–256. Lima: Consejo Nacional de
         Ciencias y Tecnología.
1996   "Acerca de dos quipus con características numéricas excepcionales."
         Bulletin de l'Institut Français d'Etudes Andines 25, no. 2: 187–202.
1997   "Los quipus con cuerdas entorchadas." In *Arqueología, antropología e
         historia en los Andes: Homenaje a María Rostworowski,* edited by Rafael
         Varón Gabai and Javier Flores Espinoza, 187–198. Lima: Instituto
         de Estudios Peruanos.
2001   "Notas sobre el descubrimiento de la clave numeral de los quipus
         incaicos." *Boletín del Museo de Arqueología y Antropología* 4, no. 5:
         115–123.

Petersen, James B., and Jack A. Wolford
2000   "Spin and Twist as Cultural Markers: A New England Perspective
         on Native Fiber Industries." In *Beyond Cloth and Cordage: Archaeo-
         logical Textile Research in the Americas,* edited by Penelope B. Drooker
         and Laurie D. Webster, 101–118. Salt Lake City: University of Utah
         Press.

Pizarro, Hernando
1920   *A los Señores Oydores de la Audiencia Real de Su Magestad.* In *Informa-*
[1533]   *ciones sobre el antiguo Perú,* edited by Horacio H. Urteaga, 16–180.
         Colección de Libros y Documentos Referentes a la Historia del Perú
         3 (Second Series). Lima: Imprenta y Librería Sanmartí.

Platt, Tristan
1986   "Mirrors and Maize: The Concept of *Yanantin* among the Macha
         of Bolivia." In *Anthropological History of Andean Polities,* edited by
         John V. Murra, Nathan Wachtel, and Jacques Revel, 228–259. Cam-
         bridge: Cambridge University Press.
1987   "Entre *Ch'axwa* y *Muxsa:* Para una historia del pensamiento político
         aymara." In *Tres reflexiones sobre el pensamiento andino,* edited by Terese
         Bouysse-Cassagne et al., 61–132. La Paz: HISBOL.
2002   "'Without Deceit and Lies': Variable *Chinu* Readings during a
         Sixteenth-Century Tribute-Restitution Trial." In *Narrative Threads:*

Accounting and Recounting in Andean Khipu, edited by Jeffrey Quilter and Gary Urton, 225–265. Austin: University of Texas Press.

Pomorska, Krystyna, and Stephen Rudy, eds.
1985   *Roman Jakobson: Verbal Art, Verbal Sign, Verbal Time.* Oxford: Basil Blackwell.

Quilter, Jeffrey, and Gary Urton, eds.
2002   *Narrative Threads: Accounting and Recounting in Andean Khipu.* Austin: University of Texas Press.

Quispe-Agnoli, Rocío
2000   *La escritura: Remedio contra la violencia. "Nueva corónica y buen gobierno" en el discurso colonial hispanoamericano.* Ann Arbor: UMI Dissertation Series.

Radicati di Primeglio, Carlos
1964   *La "seriación" como posible clave para descifrar los quipus extranumerales.* Biblioteca de la Sociedad Peruana de Historia, Serie Monografías, 6. Lima: Universidad Nacional Mayor de San Marcos.
1979   *El sistema contable de los incas.* Lima: Librería Studium.
1990   "Tableros de escaques en el antiguo Perú." In *Quipu y yupana,* edited by Carol Mackey et al., 219–234. Lima: Consejo Nacional de Ciencias y Tecnología.

Rappaport, Joanne, and Tom Cummins
1994   "Literacy and Power in Colonial Latin America." In *Social Construction of the Past: Representation as Power,* edited by George C. Bond and Angela Gilliam, 89–109. London and New York: Routledge.
1998   "Between Images and Writing: The Ritual of the King's *Quillca.*" *Colonial Latin American Review* 7, no. 1: 7–32.

Reichel-Dolmatoff, Gerardo
1949–   *The Kogi: A Tribe of the Sierra Nevada de Santa Marta, Colombia.*
1950   Vol. 1. Translated by Sydney Muiden for Human Relations Area Files, New Haven, Conn. Vol. 1 of the original Spanish edition was issued as Vol. 4, Nos. 1–2 of the *Revista del Instituto Etnológico Nacional de Colombia* (Bogotá).

Ritner, Robert K.
1996   "Egyptian Writing." In *The World's Writing Systems,* edited by Peter T. Daniels and William Bright, 73–84. New York and Oxford: Oxford University Press.

Rowe, Ann Pollard
1997   "Inca Weaving and Costume." *The Textile Museum Journal* 34/35: 5–53.

Rowe, John H.
1985   "Probanza de los incas nietos de conquistadores." *Histórica* 9, no. 2: 193–245.

Ruiz Estrada, Arturo
1981   *Los quipus de Rapaz.* Huacho, Peru: Centro de Investigación de Cien-
        cia y Tecnología de Huacho, Universidad Nacional "José Faustino
        Sánchez Carrión."
1998   "Los quipus funerarios de Cuspón." *Boletín del Museo de Arqueología
        y Antropología, Universidad Nacional Mayor de San Marcos* 1, no. 8:
        12–18.

Salomon, Frank
2001   "How an Andean 'Writing without Words' Works." *Current Anthro-
        pology* 42, no. 1: 1–27.
2002   "Patrimonial Khipu in a Modern Peruvian Village: An Introduc-
        tion to the '*Quipocamayos*' of Tupicocha, Huarochirí." In *Narrative
        Threads: Accounting and Recounting in Andean Khipu,* edited by
        Jeffrey Quilter and Gary Urton, 293–319. Austin: University of
        Texas Press.

Sampson, Geoffrey
1985   *Writing Systems: A Linguistic Introduction.* Stanford: Stanford Uni-
        versity Press.

Sarmiento de Gamboa, Pedro
1999   *History of the Incas.* Translated and edited with notes and an introduc-
[1572] tion by Sir Clements Markham. Mineola, N.Y.: Dover Publications.
        Originally published by the Hakluyt Society, Cambridge: Cambridge
        University Press, 1907.

Scancarelli, Janine
1996   "Cherokee Writing." In *The World's Writing Systems,* edited by
        Peter T. Daniels and William Bright, 587–592. New York and
        Oxford: Oxford University Press.

Schele, Linda
1994   *Maya Glyphs: The Verbs.* Austin: University of Texas Press.

Schmandt-Besserat, Denise, vol. ed.
1990   *Visible Language* 24, no. 1.
1996   *How Writing Came About.* Austin: University of Texas Press.

Scott, James C., John Tehranian, and Jeremy Mathias
2002   "The Production of Legal Identities Proper to States: The Case of
        the Permanent Family Surname." *Comparative Studies in Society and
        History* 44, no. 1: 4–44.

Scott, Norman R.
1985   *Computer Number Systems and Arithmetic.* Englewood Cliffs, N.J.:
        Prentice-Hall.

Seiler-Baldinger, Annemarie
1994   *Textiles: A Classification of Techniques.* Bathurst, Australia: Crawford
        House Press.

Sempat Assadourian, Carlos
2002   "String Registries: Native Accounting and Memory According to
         the Colonial Sources." In *Narrative Threads: Accounting and Re-
         counting in Andean Khipu,* edited by Jeffrey Quilter and Gary Urton,
         119–150. Austin: University of Texas Press.

Shady, Ruth, Joaquín Narváez, and Sonia López
2000   "La antigüedad del uso del *quipu* como escritura: Las evidencias de la
         Huaca San Marcos." *Boletín del Museo de Arqueología y Antropología,
         Universidad Nacional Mayor de San Marcos* 3, no. 10: 2–23.

Skidmore, Arthur
1981   "Peirce and Semiotics: An Introduction to Peirce's Theory of Signs."
         In *Semiotic Themes,* edited by Richard T. de George, 33–50. Human-
         istic Studies No. 53. Lawrence: University of Kansas Publications.

Soto Flores, Froilan
1950–   "Los kipus modernos de la comunidad de Laramarca." *Revista del*
1951   *Museo Nacional, Lima* 19–20: 299–306.

Spence, Jonathan D.
1984   *The Memory Palace of Matteo Ricci.* New York: Viking.

Stern, Steve J.
1986   *Peru's Indian Peoples and the Challenge of Spanish Conquest.* Madison
         and London: University of Wisconsin Press.

Street, Brian
1984   *Literacy in Theory and Practice.* Cambridge: Cambridge University
         Press.

Taylor, Gerald
1976   "*Camay, Camac,* et *Camasca* dans le manuscrit Quechua de Huaro-
         chirí." *Journal de la Société des Américanistes* 63: 231–244.

Taylor, Insup, and David R. Olson
1995   *Scripts and Literacy: Reading and Learning to Read Alphabets, Syl-
         labaries, and Characters.* Dordrecht, Boston, and London: Kluwer
         Academic Publishers.

Tedlock, Dennis
1983   *The Spoken Word and the Work of Interpretation.* Philadelphia: Univer-
         sity of Pennsylvania Press.

Tello, Julio C.
1937   "La civilización de los incas." In *Letras,* a publication of the Facul-
         tad de Filosofía, Historia y Letras of the Universidad Mayor de San
         Marcos, Lima.

Thompson, J. Eric S.
1991   *A Catalog of Maya Hieroglyphs.* Norman and London: University of
[1962]   Oklahoma Press.

Threatte, Leslie
1996   "The Greek Alphabet." In *The World's Writing Systems,* edited by
        Peter T. Daniels and William Bright, 271–280. New York and
        Oxford: Oxford University Press.

Tomic, Olga Miseska
1989   *Markedness in Synchrony and Diachrony.* Berlin and New York: Mou-
        ton de Gruyter.

Treitler, Leo
1981   "Oral, Written, and Literate Process in the Transmission of Medieval
        Music." *Speculum* 56, no. 3: 471–491.

Uhle, Max
1990   "Un kipu moderno procedente de Cutusuma, Bolivia." In *Quipu*
[1940] *y yupana,* edited by Carol Mackey et al., 127–134. Lima: Consejo
        Nacional de Ciencias y Tecnología.

Urton, Gary
1988   *At the Crossroads of the Earth and the Sky: An Andean Cosmology.*
[1981] Austin: University of Texas Press.
1990   *The History of a Myth: Pacariqtambo and the Origin of the Inkas.*
        Austin: University of Texas Press.
1992   "Communalism and Differentiation in an Andean Community." In
        Andean Cosmologies through Time: Persistence and Emergence, edited by
        Robert V. H. Dover, Katherine E. Seibold, and John H. McDowell,
        229–266. Bloomington: Indiana University Press.
1993   "Contesting the Past in the Peruvian Andes." In *Mémoire de la tra-
        dition,* edited by Aurore Becquelin and Antoinette Molinié, 107–
        144. Recherches Thématiques No. 5. Nanterre, France: Société
        d'Ethnologie.
1994   "A New Twist in an Old Yarn: Variation in Knot Directionality in the
        Inka *Khipus." Baessler-Archiv,* Neue Folge, Band 42: 271–305.
1997   *The Social Life of Numbers: A Quechua Ontology of Numbers and Phi-
        losophy of Arithmetic.* Austin: University of Texas Press.
1998   "From Knots to Narratives: Reconstructing the Art of Historical
        Record-Keeping in the Andes from Spanish Transcriptions of Inka
        Khipus." Ethnohistory 45, no. 3: 409–438.
2001   "A Calendrical and Demographic Tomb Text from Northern Peru."
        Latin American Antiquity 12, no. 2: 127–147.
2002   "Recording Signs in Narrative-Accounting Khipu." In *Narrative
        Threads: Accounting and Recounting in Andean Khipu,* edited by
        Jeffrey Quilter and Gary Urton, 171–196. Austin: University of
        Texas Press.
n.d.a   "A History of Studies of Andean Knotted-String Records." In *Guide
        to Documentary Sources for Andean Art History and Archaeology,* edited
        by Joanne Pillsbury. Washington, D.C.: Center for Advanced Study
        in the Visual Arts. In press.

n.d.b   "A Possible Tributary *Khipu* from Arica, Chile, in the Museo Chileno
         de Arte Precolombino." Manuscript.

Utaker, Arild
1974   "On the Binary Opposition." *Linguistics* 134: 73–93.

van Schooneveld, C. H.
1977   "By Way of Introduction: Roman Jakobson's Tenets and Their Poten-
         tial." In *Roman Jakobson: Echoes of His Scholarship,* edited by Daniel
         Armstrong and C. H. van Schooneveld, 1–11. Lisse, The Nether-
         lands: Peter de Ridder Press.

Vargas Ugarte, Rubén
1959   *Historia de la Iglesia en el Perú.* Vol. 2 (1570–1640). Burgos, Spain:
         Aldecoa.

von Hagen, Adriana
2000   "Nueva iconografía chachapoyas." *Iconos: Revista Peruana de Conser-
         vación, Arte y Arqueología* 4: 8–17.

von Hagen, Adriana, and Sonia Guillén
1998   "Tombs with a View." *Archaeology* 51, no. 2: 48–54.

Vorob'ev, N. N.
1961   *Fibonacci Numbers.* Translated from the Russian by Halina Moss.
         N.p.: Pergamon Press.

Waanders, Frederik M. J.
1992   "Greek." In *Indo-European Numerals,* edited by Jadranka Gvozdano-
         vic, 369–388. Berlin and New York: Mouton de Gruyter.

Wassén, Henry
1990   "El antiguo ábaco peruano según el manuscrito de Guaman Poma."
[1931]   In *Quipu y yupana,* edited by Carol Mackey et al., 205–218. Lima:
         Consejo Nacional de Ciencias y Tecnología.

Waugh, Linda R.
1982   "Marked and Unmarked: A Choice between Unequals in Semiotic
         Structure." *Semiotica* 38, nos. 3/4: 299–318.
1985   "The Poetic Function and the Nature of Language." In *Roman Jakob-
         son: Verbal Art, Verbal Sign, Verbal Time,* edited by Krystyna Pomorska
         and Stephen Rudy, 143–168. Oxford: Basil Blackwell.

Wilks, Yorick A., Brian M. Slator, and Louise M. Guthrie
1996   *Electric Words: Dictionaries, Computers, and Meanings.* Cambridge,
         Mass., and London, England: MIT Press.

Yates, Frances A.
1966   *The Art of Memory.* Chicago and London: University of Chicago
         Press.

Zamora, Margarita
1988   *Language, Authority, and Indigenous History in the "Comentarios Reales de los Incas."* Cambridge: Cambridge University Press.

Zuidema, R. Tom
1964   *The Ceque System of Cuzco.* Leiden, The Netherlands: E. J. Brill.
1982   "Bureaucracy and Systematic Knowledge in Andean Civilization." In *The Inca and Aztec States, 1400–1800,* edited by G. A. Collier, R. I. Rosaldo, and J. D. Wirth, 419–458. New York: Academic Press.
1989   "A Quipu Calendar from Ica, Peru, with a Comparison to the Ceque Calendar from Cuzco." In *World Archaeoastronomy,* edited by Anthony F. Aveni, 341–351. Cambridge: Cambridge University Press.

Index